My Visit with God

Paige Coffey

Dedication

"Then Jesus said, 'Come to me, all of you who are weary and carry heavy burdens, and I will give you rest.'"
Matthew 11:28 NLT

This book has been years in the making. It has not been easy to write as I have faced much opposition, doubt, and diversion. But through the years I have had a great support system. My mother stood by me through thick and thin. When others doubted, she believed; when others weren't supportive, she supported. And when the odds were not in my favor, she reminded me of her prayers and petitions before the Lord.

To my Aunt Brenda, who supported me financially through some of the most difficult years - thank you. She has cheered me on from the sidelines and believed in me each step of the way.

To my children, you are my heart and the reason I can face each day with a fervent resolve. You are my little pebbles, my little stones. I want you to see the works of the Lord come to pass. My children have heard me share God's messages, but they have yet to see the fullness of His promises spoken so long ago. I want them to experience the goodness of God that I have. I want them to know His life within them and His love that abounds. My prayer is that this story will forever live in their hearts as a testament to His saving grace.

To my dear husband, Doug, I want to say thank you for spurring me to action. If not for Doug, this book wouldn't be complete. He was the man without a face in 2002 that I wouldn't meet until 2018. He completes me in every way. He is my earthly strong tower and the best husband a woman could have! Thank you for believing in the gifts God has placed in me. Your consistency is profound. Thank you for your love and support, no matter what.

A Note from the Author

"Jesus told them, 'Don't let anyone mislead you,
for many will come in my name, claiming, "I am the
Messiah." They will deceive many. And you will hear of
wars and threats of wars, but don't panic. Yes, these things
must take place, but the end won't follow immediately.
Nation will go to war against nation, and kingdom against
kingdom. There will be famines and earthquakes in many
parts of the world. But all this is only the
first of the birth pains, with more to come.'"
Matthew 24:4-8 NLT

Regardless of one's personal beliefs -- faith in God or a transcendent being, something or someone greater than oneself -- we cannot deny the drastic increase of recorded testaments of encounters between human beings and the supernatural realm each year. With the Internet allowing interconnectivity and the ease in which information can be shared, we have benefited from the greatest technological leap in history, giving rise to *speculation*. Unfortunately, many people accept *speculation* at face value and consider it *knowledge*. Just go to your laptop, type "supernatural experience" into your search engine, and enter. Returned to your computer screen are lists after lists of such encounters. My assumption is there are millions of these testimonies. But can they all be true?

The words of Jesus in the Olivet Discourse in Matthew 24:4-8 (see above) forewarn us to not believe everything we hear [and read]. Instead, we should test every spirit. Could we be living in the time God referred to as ". . . until the time of the end, when many will rush here and there, and knowledge will increase" (Daniel 12:4 NLT)? Many prophecies have yet to be fulfilled before the Second Coming of Christ, but the nefariousness of that time is certainly pointing to the present day. Joel prophesied the Holy Spirit would pour himself out upon those you would least expect: "Then, after doing all those things, I will pour out my Spirit upon all people. Your sons and daughters will prophesy. Your old men will dream dreams, and your young men will see visions" (Joel 2:28 NLT). Many in the evangelical world claim we are living in this time.

Unfortunately, I knew none of this in June of 2002. I knew nothing of Paul's statement regarding God's use of the foolish to confound the wise. And with my sinful past and life riddled with bad decisions, I never thought God would waste one minute on me. But June 2002 is when God took the time to visit a low-caliber person like me. At that point in my journey, I had not read the Bible, nor did I fully believe it to be anything other than an epic story written to help Christians get through life. When the veil covering my eyes was finally removed, it was reaffirmed that God Almighty had visited me in 2002.

Every day, I would relive His visit. When I finally read the Bible, I was ecstatic to discover many parallels to what happened to me. Thankfully, these discoveries were subsequent to sharing with my Southern Baptist pastor. There was a strange look on his face as he tried explaining the experience as a long dream or something neurologically unexplainable. Without realizing, he spoke a powerful curse over me which I later had to break by the power and knowledge of the Holy Spirit.

My pastor said, "Paige, girls like you don't usually make it. You are one of the lucky ones, but you will have a hard life for sure. Jesus will see you through every step of the way, but because of your family history, this is just the way it goes." If I had only known then what I know now!

If you are choosing to read about my encounter with our holy, multifaceted Trinitarian God, then He has led you to it. Know this: What happened to me could also happen to you. We must be careful to not accept just anything we hear or read. Instead, we must test it by scrubbing it against scripture to ensure it aligns. So, if you desire to learn more about:

- God, keep reading
- the supernatural realm, keep reading
- how God interacts with His people, keep reading

I pray your desire for the Truth will blossom into a deeper spiritual quest and a longing for God in your heart. There are a multitude of other divine encounters you could choose to read, but my visit with God is absolute and true. There may be skeptics who just won't believe; instead, they will choose the easier path, which is not to believe anything unless it can be seen. They will conclude I was having withdrawal symptoms or hallucinations, but let me say this. For those who have walked closely with God, they will see Him, feel His presence, and know my testament is true.

During an interview in 2012, which I had with the *700 Club,* I was asked, "How did you know it was God and not an Angel of Light?" Without hesitation, my reply was, "I just knew!" It will be hard for some to understand and even believe, but with every fiber of my being, I never doubted it was El Shaddai, "God Almighty," speaking to me. **So, now my sole purpose in life is to inspire others with the message of hope I was given.** As a vessel, it is for no other reason but to give glory to the Lord. Jesus chose a broken little girl with nothing more to offer than two willing hands and a heart transformed by the Holy Spirit.

This testimony will shed light on the Lord's abundant

grace and unparalleled mercy. Although the visitation occurred in June of 2002, I was not able to fully share it for years afterward. My family thought I was crazy, even to the point of trying to have me committed to our local mental hospital. The friends I had at that time were convinced I had been abducted or hit my head really hard. And my soon-to-be husband was left to reconcile how the woman he had come to know so well, suddenly would not stop talking about God.

The years that followed consisted of many highs and lows. I spent my days trying to recapture every moment with God. It was the most profound experience, coupled with mystery, that left me perplexed with a giant question mark. Why? Although I asked God why He came to me, I did not understand most of what I was shown. Year after year more understanding has come to me, and I am still discovering clues to what the different scenes, words, and stories foretold. However, it finally occurred to me God was saving it for an appointed time in order to establish the foundation on which I now stand. I have learned to be patient and wait for His perfect timing.

Since that time, the subsequent testing, development, and discipline over the years have allowed for my spiritual maturity. I also have learned what "nor cast your pearls before swine" really meant. If it were not for the pain and suffering, I would not have the message of hope. Everyone has pain at some point in his / her life, but thank God, He translated mine into something beautiful, and He will do the same for you if you allow Him.

Am I worthy of your time to read this book? No, I'm not; but simply put, worthiness has nothing to do with it. Prior to my visitation, I longed to learn more about our great God. In this book, I intend to provide for those who are longing as I did for more of Him – His brilliance, His majesty, His wit, His charm,

His character, His interaction, and most importantly, His love. Truly, the Trinity is like a flawless diamond. When jewelers peer through a loop, they can see facets of a diamond not visible to the naked eye. For a week and a half during God's visit, it was as though I was the jeweler. He allowed me to peer through His loop and view the many facets of the most mysterious, largest, and most valuable diamond imaginable.

To that end, I pray, "The LORD bless you and protect you; the LORD make his face shine on you and be gracious to you; the LORD look with favor on you and give you peace" (Numbers 6:24-26 CSB).

Paige Coffey

Prologue

"What is your name!" There was a pause and the silence was deafening. The demented eyes looked back at me in disgust.

"What is your name spirit?" Then I saw that textbook smirk that accompanies this demon as it gazed back at me. "You know my name," whispered the spirit with her prideful look.

"Of course, I know your name, but I want to hear it from you!"

Then, with an all too familiar scowl, she retorted, "I am Jezebel!" Her eyes burned upon my gaze as I peered deep into Sally's soul.

Sally, a former Satanist turned Christian, struggled in all areas of her walk with Christ. She was battling a periodic opioid addiction, could not hold down a job, and struggled to find a man who would love her the right way. She had reached out to me, seeking deliverance, because nothing her previous pastors said or did helped her. Desperately seeking total freedom, she had spent countless hours in scripture, prayer and fasting, but to no avail. She had always thought she may be demonized, but her pastors informed her that a Christian could not be indwelt by demons.

Sally had heard from a close friend that I could help her achieve the freedom she so desperately wanted to experience. She knew this was the precipice in her journey with God, and fully understood what Jesus meant when He said in John 10:10, "The enemy came to steal, kill, and destroy." Sally wanted to procure the abundant life that Jesus died to give her.

"What is your legal right to this woman?", I sternly asked,

watching every shift in her rebellious stare.

"I don't have to answer you!"

"You do have to answer me spirit! Every knee shall bow and every tongue will confess that Jesus Christ is Lord! I come to you through the authority and power of Jesus Christ! Lie not to the Holy Spirt!!"

The demon writhed at even the slightest mention of Jesus, as I continued to press in regarding its legal right to Sally. After a period of silence, the demon responded with a hiss, "I do not have a legal right. It's just that no one has found me yet!"

"Then, you will have to leave, Spirit!"

At once, my prayer partner and I commanded the demon to return to the Pit. Sally groaned, her eyes rolled back, and her body shook violently until finally- the spirit released her. She fell to the floor in relief. Her tears exemplified the freedom she had finally attained after all her years in bondage.

As my prayer partner was comforting her, I stepped out of the room and with a full heart, praised the Lord for His victory. I walked over to the window and began to reflect on my own personal journey. I pondered the trauma I had experienced throughout my life and the freedom Christ had given me. If it had not been for the transformative power of the cross, I would not be where I am today. Assisting others in their healing and freedom in Christ would not be the same. I thought back to my bloodline and where the enemy first entered, and that unforgettable time when my visit with God began.

Table of Contents

Dedication
A Note from the Author
Prologue

Section One – The Backstory: Paige Coffey Before God's Visit
Chapter 1: Targets of Evil   1
Chapter 2: The Dashing Pharmacist   4
Chapter 3: Damaging Dysfunction   6
Chapter 4: Marked from Birth   11
Chapter 5: An Innocent Perception of Church   15
Chapter 6: Little Naïve Savior   19
Chapter 7: A Wolf in Sheep's Clothing   22
Chapter 8: Living a Dual Life   24
Chapter 9: The Mask   29
Chapter 10: Abusive Patterns, Ironic Parallels   33
Chapter 11: A Daughter is Born   42
Chapter 12: Someone to Lean On   46

Section Two -- What I Experienced During My Visit with God
Chapter 13: The Voices   49
Chapter 14: June 7, 2002   52
Chapter 15: Highway to Hell   57
Chapter 16: The Fear of Reverence   62
Chapter 17: Connecting the Points   65
Chapter 18: Heaven or Nothing   71
Chapter 19: The Good News   74
Chapter 20: Rewiring with Love   80
Chapter 21: Releasing the Trauma   83

Chapter 22: Confession with Peace   88

Chapter 23: After the Rewiring   92

Chapter 24: God is Love   97

Chapter 25: Share the Good News   99

Chapter 26: My Broken Heart   101

Chapter 27: The Vine   106

Chapter 28: The 700 Club   108

Chapter 29: Seminary or Bust   112

Chapter 30: Groundbreaking   116

Chapter 31: Divine Appointment   122

Chapter 32: God's Providence   124

Chapter 33: Jezebel Calling   130

Chapter 34: Counseling 101   135

Chapter 35: Healing with Hope   138

Chapter 36: Penny Lover   140

Chapter 37: Going to the Courthouse   143

Chapter 38: NUMA   146

Chapter 39: Fear of the Lord   150

Chapter 40: Sanctification   153

Conclusion

Epilogue   157

The Backstory:
Paige Coffey Before God's Visit

Chapter 1

Targets of Evil

"Yet what we suffer now is nothing compared to
the glory he will reveal to us later."
Romans 8:18 NLT

The women in my maternal bloodline were targets of evil, enduring traumatic childhoods, which prevented them from fully knowing the power of the Holy Spirit that is given freely through Jesus Christ. My great grandmother, Minnie Queen, was "saved" and attended church, but she was limited in her ability to fully know the power of the Holy Spirit in her life as a believer. She knew a lot about Jesus Christ and the cross, but she never knew or experienced the power of the Holy Spirit because she was bound by doctrine in the Southern Baptist Church.

Grandma Connie, whom I called Grandma Jones, always carried a lot of pain and other people's burdens. I could detect it in her eyes when she looked at me. She would tell me how much she loved me, yet, I could tell she never loved herself. Alcohol was a crutch for her during a large part of her life as it helped to mask the pain, shame, and sorrow. She never wanted her photos taken and would turn her head when she walked by a mirror. I learned the root of her shame later in my life. She was raped by an older brother in the fields of the family farm. Later I learned this may have continued for years and may have been why she left home as soon as she could find an escape. Though she tried traditional counseling; it only triggered the memories instead of healing the mortal wound inside. Binge drinking seemed to follow her sessions.

Thankfully, she stopped drinking when I was in elementary school. Grandma Jones was determined to make significant changes in her lifestyle to improve her health. Unfortunately, that never happened. Even up until the week before she passed, she said she was going to start doing things differently.

Grandma Jones sacrificed her life to serve everyone else. Being one of twelve children, nine of which were alive when Minnie Queen needed full-time care, her siblings were ready to place her in a nursing home, to whom she replied, "Not on my watch." In the end, she spent the last twenty years of Minnie Queen's life caring for her seven days a week, twenty-four hours a day. This is only one example of her life-long self-sacrifice.

My grandfather owned and operated two restaurants; however, he was diagnosed with tuberculosis, which required a nine-month stay at the Black Mountain Sanitarium. During this time, Grandma Jones went to work at a restaurant to earn money for the family. The alcoholism worsened, and the children wound up staying long periods alone at home.

As the youngest child, it didn't take long for my mother to realize her family looked nothing like other families. Although they went to church, she had a horrible experience when Mom and her siblings were singled out as the impoverished children. Instead of discretely aiding financially for Christmas one year, they brought the children to the front of the church to present them with presents. Mom knew exactly what they were doing. She felt deep shame, and I believe this turned her away from church for many years. I suppose the church overlooked Jesus saying, "When you give to the needy, don't let your left hand know what your right hand is doing" (Mat. 6:3 NIV). Grandma Jones, Mom, and eventually I, would all have to fight the spirit of shame.

Mom sought ways to escape the alcoholism, gloom, and the stigma under which she lived. At fifteen years of age, my mother would ride her bicycle to the neighborhood pharmacy to work behind the counter serving ice cream. She was petite, with long sandy-blonde hair and bright blue eyes, and she already had developed a nice figure. So, with these cumulative factors mounting, it seemed inescapable that Mom would become a target of evil. Tragically, she turned out to be another victim of sexual abuse while attending a teenage party. Soon after this shameful experience, Mom married her first husband, but was separated from him by the time she was sixteen.

Unfortunately, as targets of evil, the women of my bloodline never learned how to walk in the authority Christ died to give them. Knowing God was not enough. They had to know how to fight using the mighty weapons of warfare bequeathed to us through Christ's death on the cross. With that said, neither Grandma Jones nor my mother could fathom this same tragedy would one day happen to me – a granddaughter and daughter of the same bloodline. Yes, the enemy thought he had us behind lock and key.

Chapter 2

The Dashing Pharmacist

"You made all the delicate, inner parts of my body
and knit me together in my mother's womb.
Thank you for making me so wonderfully complex!
Your workmanship is marvelous—how well I know it."
Psalm 139: 13-14 NLT

Mom continued to ride her bike to work each day to the neighborhood pharmacy where she dished up ice cream concoctions. Like many other women, she was attracted to the dashing, tall pharmacist with blonde hair who would later become my father. Everyone knew he was wealthy and owned a collection of brand-new Corvettes. His popularity made his home the weekend party stop for locals. So, it was only natural that he was at the center of the town ladies' interest and gossip. At thirty two he was known as a playboy who was impossible to tie down. He could have had any one in the town, which he often did.

My dad's mother was a grammar teacher. She was very proper, attended country club events and gatherings, always wore dresses and used proper etiquette. His father was a medical doctor, who made house calls and would do so not long before he passed away from lung cancer. He was known as one of the most genuine, humble, and kind souls you could ever meet.

Little by little, mom (17 at the time) became the focus of my dad's passion. He desperately wanted to become a father and had chosen my mother as the perfect candidate to have his child. He wanted a little girl, but he would have been happy with a boy, too. Mom, who was easily lured by his charms, became enamored with him even though he was fifteen years her senior. Thus, a relationship developed, and she moved in with him.

After they realized their inability to conceive, he was diagnosed with a low sperm count. But being intensely determined, he began having fertility treatments over a period of one year. Finally, they received a positive test result. They were quite elated and relieved to learn Mom was pregnant. At least they were initially until doubts in his ability to father a child overwhelmed him – even though he'd had fertility treatments.

During her entire pregnancy, dad struggled with doubt. He couldn't accept the fact he had impregnated her, so he never bought her maternity clothes or supported her. Grandma Jones cared for her even though Mom lived with him, ensuring she had all that was needed for a successful and comfortable pregnancy.

Even when Mom went into labor, he still doubted she was pregnant with his child. He drove her to the hospital and left. As the owner and operator of the local pharmacy, closing for the day wasn't a remote consideration. Therefore, he wasn't present for my birth.

I was a Bicentennial baby born in 1976, who also served as my father's birthday present that year. When he saw me, I had blue eyes as most babies do, so he thought I might be his after all. But after a short while when my blue eyes changed as most babies' eyes do – only mine were brown and my parents both had blue eyes -- he requested a DNA test.

My father was ecstatic to learn the DNA test was positive. That's when I officially became Daddy's A number 1. That's when I officially became my father's daughter.

Chapter 3

Damaging Dysfunction

"Commit your actions to the Lord,
and your plans will succeed."
Proverbs 16:3 NLT

With the DNA test in hand, Dad was, as the cliché goes, "tickled pink." Throughout my life, my parents' running joke has been that it is impossible for me to have brown eyes. They placed the label "enigma" on me.

Many years later, my daughter studied genetics in school and told me, "Mom, with brown eyes, it is impossible for you to belong to Nana and Grandpa."

"Well," I assured her, "We had a DNA test done and if the probability for me to have brown eyes is less than 99.9%, It is an enigma. I am an enigma."

Right out of our familial starting gate, there was another hurdle to leap – another dysfunction to overcome. When Mom left her first husband at age sixteen, she never obtained an official divorce; therefore, she still had the surname of her first husband when I was born. This meant the name on my birth certificate belonged to her first husband. As a result, my biological father had to adopt me in order to change my surname to his.

Mom hoped Dad would marry her right away, but instead, she continued being what she was to him prior to my birth: his cook, maid, babysitter, and sexual partner. But Dad didn't change his established ways. He continued to play the field, and did whatever he wanted to do. In addition, Dad suffered from two addictions. The first was his work. He was a workaholic. The second was the disease, or rather a spirit, of alcoholism.

With such a promising life, he was a functioning alcoholic. He would work all day until closing, arrive home, and begin drinking until he passed out. But somehow and without exception, he'd arrive at the pharmacy the next morning at 5 o'clock to prepare the drugstore for the coming day. Tragically, he allowed his desire for mammon to supersede the law. Dad was known to be in and out of court for DUIs, selling Quaaludes to others, including undercover police officers (oops!), and having a tendency to outrun the law while impaired.

The judge explained to my Dad that if he'd settle down and get married, he would (judge) go easier on him. So, my parents married when I was two-years-old. Their union was forced, devoid of love, and short-lived. They were only together for the two years following my birth.

Mom knew Dad was not faithful. The final straw broke the proverbial camel's back when Mom was flying over a nearby town while obtaining her pilot's license during year two of their marriage. When she glanced below, her eyes focused on a yellow Corvette – her yellow Corvette – parked outside The Heart of Salisbury Motel. Instantly, she knew my father wasn't using his day off for anything other than adultery.

Sadly, the *one* memory I have of my parent's union occurred that very night. The scene is enshrined in my *Hall of Horrific Memories,* so-to-speak, as it was not only the one memory I had of them together, but it was the last memory as well. After Dad's romp at the motel, he took me to Olan Mills for a Daddy / Daughter photography session. When we arrived home, Mom was waiting. Mom was fuming. There was a confrontation; many curse words flew back and forth. The next thing I knew I was in the middle of the two of them in our hallway, screaming at the top of my lungs, "Please stop! Please, please stop!" Suddenly, Dad kicked at Mom, missed, and his foot contacted the wall instead. Both of my parents became even more enraged, and there I was with a mental video that never left my mind. It never faded. After that night, I only saw them together in the same room once more before my dad passed away in 2006. Thankfully, that was a better memory as they had gotten along well that time.

Over the years when I think of my father, I think of how he became the black sheep of his family. Grandmother never treated her middle son well. In her eyes, he just didn't fit the mold, so she pushed him aside, allowing her maids and nannies to nurture and raise him. Somehow, he was always in trouble – a rebel from birth – and only his father would come to the rescue. Grandaddy tried to fix the brokenness. Because of Grandmother's wealth and social standings, she never wanted her middle son to be the topic of conversation at Bridge Club. But much to Grandmother's denial, some suspected there were skeletons in her closet she never wanted discovered.

There was always speculation about when Grandmother got pregnant with her youngest son. The two older brothers knew he was not a Coffey. If his paternity was ever questioned by my granddaddy, no one in the family knew it. I would later learn the rest of the family always questioned it, but they never mentioned it and never whispered about the great mystery surrounding this child's conception.

You see, the word *divorce* didn't exist in my paternal family's vocabulary. So, my grandfather raised the boy as his own son even though he differed in looks from his two brothers. However, my grandparents slept in two separate bedrooms for the next thirty years.

So, when I was born, I immediately became the *red-headed step-grandchild,* which meant I'd suffer the same stigma because I was my father's daughter. Grandmother Coffey couldn't accept that my father (yes) and mother (yes) had been divorced several times. As a result, Grandmother's treatment of me was different than what she doled out to my cousins.

We only visited the Coffey family on Thanksgiving Day and Christmas Day. It was really all my dad could tolerate. One Thanksgiving after greeting me, Grandmother Coffey followed it with a conversation about my mother. This would have been fine had she proceeded with ordinary questions. Instead, in a snide tone, she asked how my mother was doing and then followed that question with, "And who is she shacking up with now?" This was, of course, in front of the rest of the family. My face immediately flushed pink. Anger welled up inside of me as I wanted to retort with something sarcastic. I was only nine years old at the time. I suppose that was my greatest moment of shame, somewhat like mom had experienced at the church a long-ago Christmas. When I wrote letters and cards to Grandmother, she would correct them grammatically and return them to me.

There is justice in this world. My uncle, the favored third son, was married for thirty-five years and had two children. Grandmother always compared me to one of his daughters, who, like me, was a dancer. But Grandmother only recognized her achievements. Eventually, my favored uncle left his wife and announced he was getting married – to a man. My cousin, to whom I'd always been compared, wound up taking a very odd path in life. It is amazing to see how things come full circle. Embarrassed, Grandmother sucked it up. She reportedly said, "I don't understand it, but I won't turn them away."

When Grandmother died, she had placed Daddy's inheritance in a trust fund. He was given an allotment each year. When my father died, my inheritance was split thirteen ways among the grandchildren and great-grandchildren. My dad's two other brother's children will be given their full share upon their father's passing. I watched as Grandmother withheld love from my dad and me but showered it upon the rest of her family. My disrespect for her was evident. Maybe splitting my inheritance was her way of letting me know she knew.

During the early stages of my sanctification process, I had a dream about her. The Lord showed me the bitterness toward her in my heart and that I must forgive her. Although forgiveness is a process, I feel as though I've come full circle and fully forgiven her.

It wouldn't have changed anything. Besides, I'd seen the writing on the wall many times. I was my father's daughter.

I believe my dad had a huge hole in his soul from the lack of mothering he was given. The pain had to be so great, it overcame any lasting joy he could have had. He placed me on a pedestal and bragged about me to everyone. But unfortunately, I wasn't enough to fill that hole.

Dad was brilliant, the most brilliant but introverted man I have ever known. He never allowed the full manifestation of God in his life to set his future ablaze by the power of the Holy Spirit. This would cost him everything in the end. He was lonely, very introverted, and a genius. Sadly, the ramifications were that his ashes never truly turned into the beauty God had wanted for him. Dad would be sober only eight years of my life.

Chapter 4

Marked from Birth

"Stand firm against him, and be strong in your faith.
Remember that your family of believers all over the world
is going through the same kind of suffering you are."
1 Peter 5:9 NIV

At times throughout my life, until my visit with God in June 2002, it seemed as though the enemy had marked me from birth. Sometimes I wondered if there wasn't a bounty on my head, considering the amount of firepower Satan sent my way. My mother once had a dream of me around the age of three.

"You were standing on a mountain," she said shuddering. "Wolves were ripping your face off, biting, and tearing at your innocent little body. All I could do was stand there and watch the gruesome scene. I was powerless. I couldn't rescue you from the attacks."

My mother and father were two of the most determined people I've ever met in my life. They had an extraordinary chip – Mom still does. Whenever they set a goal, they wouldn't just accomplish the goal, they would *SMASH* it. They would go way beyond the goal, overachieving and raising the bar each time. Some people take years to accomplish a goal. My parents were like a Navy Seal and an Olympic Athlete. I got convergence of both chips. Therefore, I believe the Lord used the fact I had to live a dual life as a child and keep a happy face throughout my training with Him. My determination and other attributes I gleaned from my bloodlines had been used by God all my young life and will be used for the rest of my life. God doesn't waste anything. He uses what the enemy has weaponized against us against the enemy. It's like a chess match, and although chess seems like a boring game, watching the Lord say "Checkmate" in the end is so worth it. I know now at forty-four why the Lord didn't just *fix* everything at once; it had to be utilized against the enemy. We will definitely talk more about this strategy later in the book.

My mother set a goal of returning to school and obtaining a nursing degree, so when she was awarded custody of me, she was able to get a job and provide for us. Whenever I visited Dad on the weekends, he rented horror movies and drank until he passed out, leaving me awake and trembling with fear from having watched the scary films. My tiny fists would beat on his chest, trying to wake him, only I failed. But no matter what Dad did, I protected him. My father never physically or sexually abused me. Even as a little girl, I realized he had demons, namely alcohol, but I never feared him. Dad never meant to intentionally hurt me. Although he was a brilliant man, he allowed the spirit of alcoholism to destroy his life.

I recall Mom dropping me off at Dad's house for a visit when I was three years old. He passed out not long after she left. Even at that age, I knew my grandma Jones' house was only four blocks away. I quietly closed the door and walked all the way to her house. I guess that is why months went by before I was able to visit Dad again.

Eventually, Dad would lose his pharmacy and license to practice pharmacology. He worked very hard to regain his license in North Carolina. He wound up going to pharmacy school twice to regain hours and recommendations. He performed community service and checked off every detail the board required in order to reinstate his license. After all was done, he was awarded license only to practice in Georgia where he graduated from the University of Georgia. Unfortunately, he was denied a license in North Carolina. I was in North Carolina. Mom never would have allowed me to go with him as she had full custody of me.

This left him spending his years in a state of deep depression and loneliness. He continued to drink until he passed out. During this time, I was exposed to Daddy's pornography magazines. He had stacks of them in his closets. I can recall how I felt when I saw those pictures. My stomach was full of nervousness, angst, and fear. It felt like something was being stolen from me. Now I know that something was my innocence.

The isolation that overpowered me felt like Dracula sucking the life out of me. As a result, the trauma I experienced at his house caused me to voluntarily cease our weekend visits. During his worst drinking binges, Dad would call me at all hours of the night, threatening to "blow his brains out," and telling me it was all my fault for leaving him alone so much. Sadly, he never realized he was missing in action for the majority of my childhood because of alcohol, drugs, and prison sentences.

The desire for my father's presence and closeness in my young life and later in my adolescence escalated in strength and neediness until it morphed into a silent desperation. But with all these emotions ever-present in my thoughts and actions, I had nowhere to turn, no one to confide in, and I was forced to push the confusion, anger, and dubious feelings downward deep inside of me. There wasn't an antidote or a known substitute in Dad's former pharmacy for the lonely desperation I hid from everyone. Unfortunately, due to his constant inebriation, I was not able to lean on my dad until I was eighteen years old when he stopped drinking.

While Mom worked third shift, I spent the nights with

Grandma Jones. She practically raised me until I was around ten years of age. My grandma was like a second mother to me. We had a lot in common. One thing is we had the same identical-colored eyes. The next thing is we shared spiritual gifts.

Years ago, after my Grandma Jones had passed, I dreamed that I was given her spiritual gifts – the ones she never opened or even realized. In the dream we were riding in a pink Lamborghini. The car represents your method of transportation in your kingdom journey and is symbolic of the level of gifting you have and where you are or where you will be in that level of gifting. To me, this was a foreshadowing of the reality to come. I was driving the car; she was my passenger. That's when I realized that I had what she never was able to realize and fully walk in during her earthly journey. Grandma Jones could have walked in so much power and authority in Christ, but sadly, she never knew it.

Think of the number of people the enemy deceives in this way. It's crazy and wonderful that I shared her eye color and her unused spiritual gifts – all rolled into one – *Me*. Grandma's unused gifts provided me with the abilities I would need in the future – the ability to lead and the ability to assist in developing others, which God led me to use for my father.

Chapter 5

An Innocent Perception of Church

"But if you cause one of these little ones who trusts in me
to fall into sin, it would be better for you to
have a large millstone tied around your neck
and be drowned in the depths of the sea."
Matthew 18:6 NLT

As a child, attending church on Sundays was a part of my life, but not always a consistent one. It was my maternal great-grandmother Minnie Queen who walked me to church when I was a little girl. She coached me to memorize certain Bible verses by having me recite them over and over to her. When Minnie Queen could no longer walk to Sunday morning services and became what the congregation calls a *shut-in*, a kind church member filled that void by delivering a taped recording of the service to her on Sunday evenings. I remember her anticipation and pleasure to be able to hear the preacher's message. Though I cannot say I listened or understood the messages, tiny seeds of the Gospel were planted in my soul and would later take root in my heart.

For me during all the years of attending church, the teachings I gleaned were that I was a horrible sinner. I'd be dammed to Hell if I didn't repent and "get saved." Every Sunday the preacher would preach a message of salvation. If I heard it once, I heard it a thousand times: "You need to *get right* with the Lord if you've sinned." I felt like I had to "get saved" every Sunday. Little by little throughout the week, I felt *unsaved* due to sin and oppression from the enemy. This was a vicious cycle and still is to this day for many Christians around the world.

Several years later, when Mom and I began attending the Lutheran church, I was confirmed, but I never understood the meaning and / or purpose of all the ceremonial stuff that accompanied confirmation. Try as I might I would fall asleep during the services because of the monotone and repetitive scriptures that we read.

Praying was foreign and something I didn't know how to do even though I did ask God to bless my family. When report cards were to be sent home, I'd ask God for straight A's – trivial nonsensical requests like this. Although I did try to pray as a child, walking with the Lord wasn't something I was taught how to do. I had no idea He'd be the one carrying me during the difficult times of my life because I believed God existed above in Heaven – not here on earth or within me. If only someone would have told me about the role of the Holy Spirit in the life of the believer. If I had only known this miraculous Third Person of the Trinity. If I had only known that He would come in and make His home inside of me, and then HE would help me overcome my propensity to sin, I would have said, "Sign me up!" Unfortunately, the very power of God, the One who is available to know personally as He leads you into all truth, would remain a mystery for many, many years of my life.

Later as a seminarian, I learned Western Christianity contributed to my misguided view of God, as well as many others who shared this same view. In Western Christianity, we are taught God is a transcendent Being, which means He is above us and outside of the material universe. Perhaps this is why I always looked up to talk to Him in prayer and have seen others doing the same. But I would learn God is both transcendent and imminent. Of the two, imminence is the missing part taught in Western Christianity. It explains how God "comes into our hearts" and lives there. His proximity is not external; it is internal. He becomes one with those who accept His grace and mercy and receive eternal salvation – those whom He saves.

Unfortunately, like many other Christians, my perceptions were that attending church on Sundays and opening my Bible to follow along with scripture references during worship services was enough. Although I attempted to read scripture, the connection was missing, so my efforts ended with naps, misunderstandings, and frustration.

As a sinful young adult with a burden of guilt weighing heavily on my shoulders, I recalled my Southern Baptist roots. Our pastor had preached the King James Version (KJV) was the only "original Bible;" therefore, all other translations were "of the devil." The minister's teachings were short and seemed certain: all other translations would be burned, and if we rebelled by reading them, we would spend eternity in Hell.

Fortunately, not all Southern Baptists believe the same way about the different translations of the Bible. My minister happened to adhere to a more strict, fundamentalist interpretation of the Baptist doctrine. Although I knew so much of their teachings was legalistic, I had no idea just how much I was conditioned by what I was first taught. According to the online Oxford Dictionaries, theological legalism means adherence to "non-biblical rules and regulations," with stress on *doing* more than *being*. Legalism is deadly and has no place in messages of grace and love.

The traditions and theological legalism from the Baptist and Lutheran Churches were ingrained in my DNA. Over the years, a great blessing for me has been to truly discover and follow the way of the Lord, not the traditions of men. Now, after my encounter with God almost twenty years ago and after graduating from seminary, I can understand why Paul required fourteen – seventeen years of preparation before the Lord fully released him into public ministry. I can't stress it enough; legalism is deadly and has no place in a message of grace and love.

Chapter 6

Little Naïve Savior

"He will wipe every tear from their eyes,
and there will be no more death or sorrow or crying or pain.
All these things are gone forever."
Revelation 21:4 NLT

At a very young age, around six or seven, my childhood was forcefully wrenched from my being. After living in two marriages devoid of love and emotional support, Mom married a man, whom she dearly loved; however, his love for cocaine superseded his love for her and God. And it was his desire for the addictive substance that ushered in extreme waves of violence and anger toward my mother and even me.

This stepdad was her third husband. He spent long nights away, mixing cocaine with alcohol. Afterwards he'd return home ready to argue, so he'd pick fights with Mom. It didn't take long before the arguments intensified and became physical. Not only were we emotionally and mentally scarred by abuse, we were physically battered and suffered greatly because of his violent, drug-infused affliction.

Hearing my mother's cries and screams from the kitchen or from their bedroom were sounds I couldn't tolerate. As I listened, I'd be mad and would grow angrier and angrier until my determination to save my mother and the fierceness I felt tossed aside any concerns about my small size or the repercussions afterward. With one jump, I'd cling to his back, while pounding and pounding his shoulders and head with tight fists. In this childish state of naiveté, my actions were protecting Mom. But in the end as I grew older, realization dawned on me: My involvement had only made it worse for her because it further increased his rage, which turned toward both of us.

He wouldn't slap or punch my body with his open hand or his fists. Instead, I'd hear the telltale sound of a leather belt whipping free from his pant belt-loops. What happened next was inevitable and something that couldn't be begged or pleaded away. He possessed no mercy, no forgiveness. He'd belt whip me until I began urinating all over myself. Finally, after it was over, Mom would throw a few things in her car, and we'd flee to his own mother's house for safety. Mom and I would pray he'd just pass out and sleep off his all-encompassing rage. On occasion, he'd follow us to his mother's house and try to continue the beatings once he arrived. Thankfully, physical and mental abuse was all the stepfather cared to share in our home. He never sexually abused me. However, his teenage son did.

The teenage boy was six years older than I was. When my stepdad and mother were asleep, he would ask me to play doctor. This was his way of convincing me that doctors must examine their patients without clothes sometimes. I'll never forget my innocence slipping away as this teenage boy fondled me and later taught me how to perform oral sex on him.

Why didn't I tell, you may ask? I knew better! He threatened to tell our parents that it was my idea or that I was lying. Whenever he'd approach me, and afterwards, I remained silent. After all, his father probably would beat my mother if I ever said anything against his son. Being all too familiar with being on the receiving end of repercussions from opening my mouth, I didn't say anything except what a seven-year-old child might say. It all boils down to this: at a young age, I'd been introduced to *fear* and *fear* was no friend, just a horrible thing Satan likes to have worm its way into our lives. Did I fear for my life? Yes. Did I fear for my mother's life? Yes. There was absolutely no way I would be the one rocking the boat more than it already had been.

Years later, after I began living my life in obedience of God, I harbored one regret: I was saddened the teenage son and I never had a *last* talk. Once the Lord began my sanctification process, part of it was forgiving everyone who had abused me. As Christians, we know bitterness touches everything. Like yeast in dough, it's like cancer to the body. As I sent letters to my abusers forgiving them for what they had done, his was the one letter that never went out.

I longed to tell my stepbrother that I'd forgiven him – no matter if he deserved my forgiveness or not – but unfortunately, he died in a tragic accident many years ago. So, I'd lost that chance to share my forgiveness with him. Even though many years have passed, and my scars have been healed by the Great Physician, I can't help but wonder what fueled his abusive actions toward me – a child of seven. Had someone sexually abused him? We'll never know, but it was sad never having resolution in that situation.

During this time of my life and throughout Mom's third marriage, Satan would loyally send a great deal of fear to abide within me. Now, I understand how fear was rooted in my soul through an abundance of ways. He had me right where he wanted me, or shall I say the enemy did.

Chapter 7

A Wolf in Sheep's Clothing

In 1989, Mom fell in love with a man whom she considered her soulmate. She met him at Phillip Morris, USA, where they both worked. He had a subtle disposition, country charm, and the willingness to become the family unit we'd longed for and desperately needed. So, after they were married, Mom and I moved from a small town in North Carolina where I had been born, and where everyone knew me as my *father's daughter*, to another small town in North Carolina, which was about forty-five minutes away. Mom thought this fourth marriage and this relocation would be the beginning of a new and wonderful life for us.

Even though this man seemed almost too good to be true, we were infatuated and optimistic in the belief we were finally going to be all right. In the church he attended, and we subsequently joined, he sang in the choir and served as a deacon. In the community, he was well-known, respected, and revered as a gentleman. We were fooled into believing this time would be different.

My stepfather's parents kept me in their home while Mom and he worked the third shift together. One memory I'll never forget is how excited my mother was when he was transferred to the day shift. Her delight was innocent, unsuspecting, as she relished the change. Her husband wouldn't be working all night and would be home with me. But when we were at home and the doors were closed, he soon revealed his true self to me: He was a wolf in sheep's clothing. I'm reminded of Psalm 10: 2-11 (NLT):

The wicked arrogantly hunt down the poor. Let them be caught in the evil they plan for others. For they brag about their evil desires; they praise the greedy and curse the Lord.

The wicked are too proud to seek God. They seem to think that God is dead. Yet they succeed in everything they do. They do not see Your punishment awaiting them. They sneer at all their enemies. they think, "Nothing bad will ever happen to us! We will be free of trouble forever!"

Their mouths are full of cursing, lies, and threats. Trouble and evil are on the tips of their tongues. They lurk in ambush in the villages, waiting to murder innocent people. they are always searching for helpless victims.

Like lions crouched in hiding, they wait to pounce on the helpless. Like hunters they capture the helpless and drag them away in nets. Their helpless victims are crushed, they fall beneath the strength of the wicked. The wicked think, "God isn't watching us! He has closed His eyes and won't even see what we do!"

The work schedule wasn't the only change for our family. This is when my life drastically changed – for the worst. Mom never could have fathomed or even considered the danger in which she was placing me.

Chapter 8

Living a Dual Life

"Get rid of all bitterness, rage, anger, harsh words, and slander, as well as all types of evil behavior. Instead, be kind to each other, tenderhearted, forgiving one another, just as God through Christ has forgiven you."
Ephesians 4: 31-32 NLT

They say hindsight is twenty-twenty, which is why I clearly can see how my stepfather groomed me from day one. Whenever Mom and my stepfather purchased lottery scratch-off tickets, I'd get so excited anticipating the pleasure I'd receive from scratching each circle to expose losses or wins. No matter how many were losses, my optimism kept me believing the next ticket would be a winner.

Unfortunately, Dad's absence from my life allowed this new stepfather to find points of contact and use emotional manipulation by trying to fill the *fatherly gap* in my heart. I've come to realize it was all part of the process pedophiles follow, so I could be used as his sexual object later.

As if it were yesterday, I remember the evening when he and I were in the living room, watching television. That's when I noticed he'd placed a stack of lottery tickets on the accent table between our two chairs. Excited, I asked if I could help scratch-off the tickets. He grasped my hand in his and placed it on his penis. "Only if you touch this first."

My stomach turned somersaults while my heart shattered. I froze with dread! In that fleeting and significant moment, all joy and hope left the room. Because of my past experiences, I was fully aware of the drill. Satan's grooming to this point of my life only padded my stepfather's evil intent.

Past traumatic events had programmed me to keep silent and not destroy my mother's happiness. My mind was like a whirlwind. How could this be? He was her soulmate. We had moved our lives to be with him in this new town, new school, and all new friends. My mother would be devastated.

But I was unaware of his intentions to make me the *mistress* of our home and then his personal prostitute. After the *lottery ticket incident* occurred, I'd awaken to find him sitting on the edge of my bed with his groping hands under the covers, trying to fondle me as long and as much with which he could get away. My mother was working third shift, so I was easy prey for this predator.

According to the 2010 online article, "Grooming: How Child Molesters Create Willing Victims" by Laurie Gray, she quotes Kenneth Lanning, a former FBI agent. "Pedophiles groom their victims. Grooming is a perversion of romantic courting." He further outlines five steps in the process:
Identify a victim
Get to know everything about the victim
Fill a need the victim has
Lower inhibitions
Initiate the abuse
(*National Assoc. of Adult Survivors of Child Abuse*, 2010).

My stepfather was a clever pedophile and had followed the process perfectly. Little had I known he was building trust with me in order to perpetuate his nasty addiction. When the sexual abuse began, he convinced me this was something separate that we did and explained it like this: "It keeps me from cheating on your mother. I've done so much for you, so this is something you can do for me."

Night after night, with familiar trepidation, I stared as Mom backed out of the driveway onto the road's pavement and headed to work. My eyes lingered even after the car was out of sight, just hoping she'd return. When this sick and devious man thought the coast was clear, he'd knock on my door, reminding me to *wash up* and bring a washcloth. He would say, "Slide in here with me in the bedroom," the one he shared with my mother.

In the beginning he performed oral sex on me and made me watch pornography while using sex toys. He worked his way up to teaching me how to perform oral sex on him. Within a few months, he stole my virginity and referred to it as *doing pretend*. This is what he called it. "We're pretending," he'd say. He certainly knew how to speak to a child. Without remorse and with pain, he stole my virginity, along with any remaining traces of childhood innocence I had left. For years to follow, he forced me sleep in the bed with him until an hour before Mom was due to return home.

There are certain triggers for me even to this day. Any time I see Tone soap, my stomach turns. You see. The washcloth wasn't just for me. It was for his smelly, uncircumcised penis. As he was teaching me how to perform oral sex on him the way he liked it, all I could smell was what I called "nasty man smell," so I washed him with the only soap we used at the time: Tone.

At first the nightly *pretending* seemed like an out of body experience. After a while, I learned to compartmentalize what we did at night from the father figure he was during the day. His sick addictions for pornography and sex toys became part of my daily life. I strongly believe I developed Stockholm syndrome, even though it was never clinically diagnosed. With this syndrome, the victim may develop feelings of trust or affection toward his / her captor. The affection wasn't a romantic one by far. You see, he went over the top to be a father figure to me, and that is what I desperately needed. The more I shut out what happened when the lights were out and my mother was gone, the easier it was to live two separate lives.

This resulted in me living a dual life, which created internal fear and constant emotional and physical pain. Being forced to live a dual life was traumatic and a millstone I internalized and carried privately for years. My negative view of life had been planted long ago, but it had never blossomed until now. This view continued through the years, becoming the catalyst for my toxic behavior, which would last until I was regenerated years later by God.

You may be asking why I didn't tell or why I didn't run to a family member? This man was so highly regarded in the community, no one would have believed me. But I knew one person who would, and that was my mother. In the beginning of his nightly rape sessions, I thought there would be an end at some point. When I realized I was trapped as his sex slave until I got out of that house, I finally developed the nerve to tell him what I was planning.

During a family trip to the local grocery, he and I were talking behind Mom. I threatened to tell her everything. He calmly replied, "You tell her, and I will kill her. Then you will have to live with what you've done." Of course, I never threatened this again because I knew in my heart, he was serious. There were no doubts. Well, that was the end of that. The look in his eyes revealed something or someone I had never met up to that point. His reputation and his status meant everything to him. We were worthless trash.

My stepfather's boldness grew to the point he'd wait for Mom to turn her back, and then he'd touch me. Our refrigerator was in the same room as the washer and dryer. He would wait until I was folding laundry or doing something out of Mom's sight to approach me. His boldness increased day after day as touching evolved to more and more depending on how long he could keep me cornered.

To this day I loathe basements and refuse to ever live in a home with a basement. When Mom left her third shift position, it became harder and harder for my stepfather to have access to me. We had a basement in this house. My stepfather would spend hours each week reloading shot gun shells in his basement workshop. He would ensure Mom was upstairs, engrossed in a television program before asking me to grab a washcloth and join him downstairs. I can remember the sound of the door creaking open and dreading what was ahead of me each and every time I had to visit his evil basement lair. As I descended the stairs, I'd think to myself, *If my mom only knew what he was doing to me right now.*

My mother loved horses. She was infatuated with them and looked forward to spending time at the barn with them during the afternoon feedings. This became his next time to make a play on me. He had it timed perfectly. He would have me perform oral sex until he ejaculated, which would require the exact amount of time Mom would spend at the barn. He was the master manipulator and often said, "Don't bite the hand that feeds you." So, I didn't.

Chapter 9

The Mask

"They don't know where to find peace
or what it means to be just and good.
They have mapped out crooked roads,
and no one who follows them
knows a moment's peace."
Isaiah 59:8 NLT

By this time in my abbreviated childhood, the treasured innocence of the little girl, whom God had created, had been spoiled and had disappeared. I was nothing like God had intended me to be; only an outer shell existed. When the overwhelming despair set in, my outer casing became even more fragile than an egg. So, to protect myself and to hide the truth of who I was, I fooled everyone by presenting them with a mask – a poor replica of whom I wished I were.

When he sensed his elaborate stories' effects on me were waning, he offered money. The first time I accepted it, that's the moment I became a prostitute in my own home. To me it seemed there was no other way out. Whenever Mom was punishing me for some infraction I'd committed, my stepfather would convince her not to ground me. Being *ungrounded* cost me additional *sessions* with him.

A *session* was the newest nomenclature that had replaced *pretending*. Regardless of what it was called, he kept a running tab of the number of sessions he was owed. Since he did the grocery shopping and cooking, I had to offer sexual favors in exchange for foods I liked. I was at the age when popularity depended on new clothes, new shoes, school parties and trips, and spending money. These equated to him paying me for sexual favors, which meant additional sessions with him. He requested extreme sexual favors and backed them with extreme payment offers. Each body part had a price. I was older at this point and all I heard from him was, "This is your choice you know. You don't have to do this." It was a lie. Everything that came out of his mouth was a lie. I hated him, and I hated every touch, every smell, every look, and every moment of my youth passing me by.

One time my stepfather invented an elaborate story that Mom had my phone tapped and was secretly keeping all the tapes of conversations I'd had with my friends. He told me, "The tapes haven't been picked up yet. I will intercept them and add extra sessions."

Coinciding at the same time, Mom quit her job at the company where she and my stepfather worked to continue her career in nursing. Unfortunately, chronic back pain affected her daily routine. As a result, Mom turned to pain killers, which easily became an addiction. Over the years, the reliance on medication made her irritable and more detached from me than ever. The bullseye target was only growing larger, so I found any and all excuses not to be alone with him.

My stepfather knew I was getting old enough to leave with friends. So, he became the coolest stepdad, allowing parties and joking and cutting up with everyone. On the outside looking in, my school friends must have thought he was the coolest and I had it all. Due to his popularity and notoriety at that time, many high school girlfriends didn't believe the truth about this monster when the truth was revealed. But this is my story to share, and I share it before God Almighty as the truth. He saw me through those years, and He will see me through this backlash when this book is released.

I could not wait to get my driver's license. I'd always shared Daddy's enthusiasm for fast cars, namely Corvettes. A car would mean the first form of escape and taste of freedom from my abuser. I began begging Mom to buy me new cars, and as a result, I became a master manipulator. At the time, I didn't realize they were peace offerings and ways to create anticipation and excitement for my dreary life. I didn't realize they were temporary band aids for the pain and anger I harbored inside.

I was usually driving the others who needed a designated driver. It was my stepdad who introduced me to pot. He thought it would help me calm down, so I wouldn't be so bothered by what he was doing to me. He also brought out pot bowls when my friends were visiting. Again, he wanted to be the *cool* Stepdad.

Smoking pot a few times along with the occasional cigarette was the extent of it for me. I swore I did not want to wind up like my parents, so I wasn't concerned about having the ability to say no. I would learn later in life that Satan always sets us up with the small, negligible choices in life. A little here and there eventually accumulates, which is how addicts end up with such nasty habits when their original intent was just occasional participation.

I was excited for high school graduation to hurry and come. With a good job and hard work, I'd be able to support myself and break free of the chains and shackles that had prohibited my escape from this abusive prison. Finally, it seemed my life would be changing for the good. I would have freedom and a big world in which I could stretch my wings and fly. As the saying goes, "the sky is the limit." But I was entering the adult world so ill-equipped. I was immature and naïve with no understanding of how a man is supposed to love and treat a woman as God intends. I lacked the ability to troubleshoot and make sound decisions. Instead, my life would be riddled with a string of bad decisions. As a result, I began following in my mother's footsteps and some of the same patterns she had devised. Looking back, we shared a lot of parallels, as well.

32

Chapter 10

Abusive Patterns, Ironic Parallels

"Direct your children onto the right path,
and when they are older, they will not leave it"
Proverbs 22:6

In the near future, I told myself, *I'll get out of here. I'll be out from under his thumb and the daily torture and abuse.* My desire was to escape from my stepfather's house as soon as possible. But regrettably, I would soon trade my current nightmare for another horrible, physically abusive relationship, which I allowed to last four years -- too long.

After graduation, my mother announced, "I'm leaving your stepdad and getting an apartment. If you want to come with me, you can." That was an easy decision for me to make. After we moved into the apartment, I felt relief for the first time I could remember. It was wonderful to breathe easily, to take a shower or bath without prying eyes and the fear of moving hands. This haven, this wonderful apartment, was what I had been wanting and praying to have for Mom and me. But my bliss was short-lived when Mom announced she was reuniting with the first man who had molested me. They were getting married. As to the abuse he had inflicted on me, he only had to tell her it didn't happen, and she believed him. Without a place to go and no money to get an apartment, I was forced to return to the home of my stepdad, my tormentor.

Nothing changed when I moved back. Everything continued – the whole ante – because for me to stay in his home, I had to pay. Acquiescing to his revolting wishes was my payment. This continued for almost a year. Then I met this guy.

It didn't take long before we were inseparable, so he asked me to move in with him. To escape the maltreatment in my daily life, I said, "Yes!" without hesitation. Six months into our relationship, he took me to Myrtle Beach. We stayed at the lovely Ocean Dunes, where his parents owned a place. One of my simple pleasures in life is being at the beach and eating pancakes at one of the many breakfast restaurants. Excited and hungry, I decided to wake him, so we could go and eat pancakes.

Unpredictably, all 6'4" of him flew out of bed in a rage and slammed me (5' 0") against the wall. He grabbed my head between his hands like a vise, banging it against the wall. But he wasn't finished until he tried to choke me. At this point in my attack, I was ballistically crying. Suddenly, he realized what he was doing and backed off.

In shock and disbelief, for the first time in my life, I watched a demon manifest before my eyes. Calmly, but still angry, he returned to the bed and laid down. His voice was menacing when he said, "I'll get up when I'm good and ready. Don't do it again." I remained silent, not saying another word. That's when the physical abuse started.

The severity of battering progressed to punching, kicking, and throwing me around. Fortunately, a couple of weeks could go by peacefully, but when he got into a rage, it would get worse and worse.

I had a really good job at a bank, until he had me fired. When I got a different job, he got angry one day and came to the office and dragged me out of the office, shoved me into the car, and drove us home. I couldn't hold down a job –

because of him.

On the night my mother was going to get married, for no reason, he flew into a rage. Of course I planned to attend her wedding. So, on the night of the wedding, while I was showering, he pulled back the curtain, turned the hot water to scalding, and sprayed me with shaving cream. He shoved me against the fiberglass bathtub wall and roughly rubbed the cream.

"You're not going anywhere. You're staying here," he hissed.

"I'm going to my mother's wedding."

"Nope, you're not."

Then he grabbed me and pulled me out of the shower. Luckily, I snatched a towel. My recollections are vague, but it seems I was wearing something – maybe I'd grasped a shirt -- before he dragged me outside. His home was in the country, surrounded by fields as far as you could see all around. He hit me a couple of times and slammed my head into the truck door's window. Then he drove me around to the back of the house. Suddenly, he whipped out a gun and held it to my head.

In a threatening voice, he said, "You know what? No one gives a - - - - about you. I could kill you and bury you right down there, and nobody would care. That's how worthless you are." The horrendous tirade continued for hours, but my shaking hands, throbbing head, and bruised body prohibited me from hearing the words. My scrambled thoughts focused on the innate desire to survive, while realizing the futility of any desire to run. With a grateful and shuddering release, we returned to the house. Maybe his rage was over. But it wasn't. He broke the coffee table, removed all the pictures from the wall, and broke them over his knees. The living room was a disaster area. I was a disaster, too.

Mom knew I had planned to attend the wedding, so she

knew something was wrong. She asked my aunt and uncle to go and check on me. When they arrived, my aunt came to the front door. He met my aunt outside; he wouldn't allow me to go outside. *This meant my uncle was downstairs!* So, I shot downstairs and hurried out the glass door. My tormentor heard me. I ran to my uncle, a former Hell's Angel. He was older since his biker days, but he was still intimidating and no one easy to deal with.

Out of the corner of my eye, I saw my boyfriend running down the sidewalk toward us. Quickly, I hugged my uncle and whispered a warning in his ear. "Don't confront him. He will kill you." I knew if there were an altercation, one of the two men would die. "Go to the end of the road and call the police now." My uncle acted as if nothing was wrong, but my aunt and boyfriend had exchanged angry words while at the front door. After my aunt and uncle left, I knew I was in for it. My heart was racing with anticipation as I begged God to send the police before he killed me. From the downstairs exit where we had been standing with them, my boyfriend dragged me by the hair of my head inside and up the stairs. With each step I could feel my scalp being separated from my skull like a rug pulled from a hardwood floor. I never knew this could happen, but for days afterward, I had *scalp knots* all over my head. It would be at least a week before they settled down, and it would take at least a year to replace the patches of missing hair.

Suddenly, I heard our Rottweilers barking. I begged and pleaded in my heart, *Please let it be them.* And it was the police.

They had pulled up the long driveway with their lights off, thank God. My heart was racing out of my chest and adrenaline was rushing through my veins like something out of a horror movie. If only I could have seen what they saw in my eyes when they looked at me. There I was, blood running down my face, arms, and legs. Dried shaving cream still covered parts of my body and hair. Everything in sight had been shattered or destroyed. Immediately they cuffed him; off to jail he went. I'll never forget his nasty words to me and the officers as they put him in the patrol car. If only my reprieve could have been permanent. The North Carolina law for domestic violence had changed, which meant the oppressor had to remain in jail until he / she could come before a judge. Thank God he wouldn't be out for a couple of days.

Do you know the saying, "an apple doesn't fall far from the tree"? Well, it applied here. He was just like his father. He'd learned the unacceptable behavior and inherited demons from his father. I would learn later his father had rendered his mother near death twice because of the beatings she'd received.

At that time, my only choice was to return to my stepdad's house. My mother had lost her apartment and was living with the man she had married that night. She was in active addiction at the time, so I received very little help from her. Dad was probably inebriated. If I went to my Grandma Jones' house, my boyfriend would follow me and cause issues there. There was no escaping this situation. What alternatives did I have?

On top of this, I received a call from his father, who was threatening me. "If you don't go to court on Monday morning and tell them it was just an issue between you two, you provoked him, and it was all your fault. You must drop the charges against him. I don't care how you do it, but you have to say, 'you are going to drop the charges.' And that is what is going to happen.'"

I did not have my father who was drunk, but had he known this at the time, he would have been in jail over it. There was no one to intervene. It was like actually living the life of the female character in *Sleeping with the Enemy* movie. So, on Monday morning, I went just as I was told to do and refused to press charges against him. Afterward, he drove me home.

There were many, many times when I'd call Mom and whisper, "Come get me. Come get me." In the middle of the night, she would creep up the driveway with her car lights off while I waited, heart racing and full of fear that any moment he would creep up behind me. This was the most trembling, horrifically quivering fear you could imagine. She would take me to my grandmother's house, as I could only stay with her so long before he'd come there and wait until I agreed to come home. I knew he'd cause a scene with my grandma; I wouldn't allow her to be hurt in any way, so I'd go back with him.

The day when I finally escaped his hold on my life, it began with us getting into some argument. Now, with him I couldn't cry, or it would make things worse. Tears infuriated him, and he'd call me *weak*. I didn't dare fight back, or it would make things worse. No matter what I did, it would make things worse.

I had a Mustang that had been built for drag racing. We participated in drag racing together. When it was possible, I grabbed my keys and ran to the car. My face was bleeding. My neck was bleeding. I jumped into the car and took off. I was driving down the long driveway to the dirt road. His grandparents lived next door. Somehow, he ran out of the house and caught up with me. He caught the back of my spoiler, and here I am, dragging him down the dirt road. I parked and quickly ran into his grandparents' house, pleading for help.

"She's just crazy," he said. "I've told you that." Apparently, he'd painted a picture of me that his grandparents believed. Dejected and afraid, into the car I went and back to the house.

But God heard my prayers. This was God all the way around.

This guy wound up talking to his ex-wife. They had been married for two years before splitting up. He knew I planned to attend college, so he continued talking to her. My stepbrother and I were able to get a place while attending Pitt Community College. Then I planned to transfer to East Carolina University. I was excited; life was great.

One weekend when my stepbrother was gone, my ex-boyfriend drove all the way to East Carolina and packed my stuff. Then he drove me back to his house. This concluded by costing me another valuable year of time. Then he started talking to his ex-wife again. Fortunately, they got back together. I moved out, got a new job, and purchased a brand new trailer. Finally on my own, I was so proud of my new home and *tickled pink* over my job and new life. But when he and his ex-wife would argue, he'd come to visit me. Repeatedly, I'd receive complaint letters from the park owners because his car was too loud. They even attempted eviction, but it didn't work. The last time he visited me there, he was raging. He entered my home, broke my table, took all my pictures from the walls, and broke them, and knocked a hole in the wall.

To summarize this relationship, I can look back and see God's providence. This man tried hard to get me pregnant. We even tried fertility testing and timed each month when I was ovulating. He desperately wanted to be a father. The reason he went back to his ex-wife was because she had a child out of wedlock who needed a father. He saw a perfect opportunity. After we finally parted ways, and he was back with her, she was pregnant with twins within months of their remarriage. Now that was such a blessing!

Justice is something the Lord has spoken to me about numerous times over the years. He told me to ask Him for justice. This relationship haunted me year after year, day after day. Later, I would learn the spirit of Legion entered through this union. It would be years before I was set free, but one thing I did receive back in 2018 was justice.

A mutual friend of ours contacted me on *Facebook*, asking if my ex-boyfriend could return something of value to me and apologize. My heart immediately began pounding as memories came flooding back. I hesitated but knew in my heart this was God granting me that for which I had asked – justice!

One summer day, my ex-boyfriend and I met where no one would suspect. He arrived just as scheduled. I was prayed up and had no fear whatsoever. Surely, he did have something of value. He found my high school annual in the back of the car he drag-raced when we were together. That was certainly no coincidence. I felt the Lord set this moment up as we both needed closure. He peered into my eyes, and with tears, he said "I want to apologize to you for everything."

With tears streaming down my face, my response was a question. I asked, "Everything? Do you really remember what you did to me? Do you remember the beatings, the blood, the words, the hate, the rage?"

"Yes, Paige," he replied. "I remember everything I did to you." After a short pause, he continued, "There isn't a day that goes by when I don't think about you and what I did to you. I am so sorry." His words seemed so genuine, so heartfelt. We both cried.

I knew he had abused his wife the first time they were together, so I asked, "Have you continued to hurt your wife?"

"Nope," he replied. "Since we got back together, I've never laid a hand on her."

"Do you know why you don't have to? She listens to you and knows her place. She is careful not to step out of bounds. You couldn't control me, and that was the problem. I was young, but I wanted to work and have a future and go to college. You didn't want that. You wanted me to be under your thumb all the time with no freedom. I lived the life of having to account for every minute if I went anywhere. You were utterly controlling. I had no life."

This moment was surreal and healing for both of us. The greatest thing that happened that day was witnessing with my own eyes how God *does* work *all* (not just some) all things together for good for those who love him and are called according to his purpose.

When this man drove away that day, my heart was brimming with joy. That's when the nightmares stopped. I was free!

Chapter 11

A Daughter is Born

"When a woman is in labor, she has pain because her time has come, but when she has given birth to a child, she no longer remembers the suffering because of the joy that a person has been born into the world."
John 16:21 CSB

It seemed impossible for me to have healthy relationships, which is why I found myself running from them once anything turned south. I lived with painful memories, unforgiveness, and shame. These remnants from my life experiences had locked my heart in a cold, dark prison. I was numb to love and trust.

After the physically abusive relationship, I moved to Charlotte, NC, where I had been hired as a data specialist. This was a new start for me in a new home but with a broken heart. Even though I knew it was divine intervention that ended the physically abusive relationship, I loved him. Living each day and knowing he had returned to his ex-wife was grueling, so to deal with the pain, I jumped into another relationship.

Little did I know that I was spiritually dead inside. I didn't know God personally at this point in my life, so I didn't know He was what I was missing, that He would fill that giant void in my heart. Like most people with unhealed trauma, I was endeavoring to fill the void or the "eternity in my heart" (Ecclesiastes. 3:11, NLT) God had supernaturally embedded with people, places, and things.

This gift of eternity from God can work against us if we aren't careful. It was what the enemy used to work against me. I filled the void only God could fill with relationships. Some people choose to fill theirs with money, materialism, sex, drugs, etc. I was sure another man would come along who would or could make me complete.

Woody Allen, the atheist filmmaker, made an insightful observation about mankind without any revelation of God:

> The universe is indifferent, so we create a fake world for ourselves, and we exist within that fake world, a world that, in face means nothing at all, when you step back. It is meaningless. But it's important that we create some sense of meaning because no perceptible meaning exists for anybody.

I was at an important crossroad during this time in my life. With the new lease on life, I had been given, I could have sought the Lord's kingdom as He instructed. "Seek the kingdom of God first and His righteousness, and then all these things will be added unto you" (Matthew 6:33, NLT). Instead, I persisted in the idolatry of fake happiness, which was yet another soon-to-be failed relationship. This one, however, brought me the first of the two greatest physical gifts I've ever received: my children.

When I met my daughter's father, I was still on the rebound from the abusive relationship. He was a friend of a friend who could dance, and I loved to dance. One night we danced together at a local Charlotte bar. From that night forward, we were an item. Three short months later, on my twenty-second birthday, I conceived my daughter. He had told me he was infertile, but he had lied. I would later learn from his father that he had intended to get me pregnant because he knew it would be the only way I would stay with him. Her father and I married, but soon afterward, I realized what a colossal mistake I had made. I tried to convince myself I would grow to love him, but now, as I look back, it's easy to realize I only married him, so I could truthfully tell our daughter she wasn't born out of wedlock

Now I understand how the curse of illegitimacy is passed from one generation to the next. I was conceived out of wedlock, and instead of waiting for the man God had for me, I settled. the curse of illegitimacy was in perpetuity, passed to my daughter. Thankfully, it has been broken. I will write more on this topic in the days to come.

When my precious daughter was born, she touched my heart in a way no one else ever could. This was proof I could love again. My baby became my *why*, my everything, giving me a new reason to live, a new reason to wake up every day, a new reason to hope. That is, until Satan made it his mission to destroy any peace or happiness I'd finally found. Although her father and I tried to make a go of it, I never could love him as he deserved, so I promised myself I would leave when our daughter was two years-old.

On her second birthday, I kept the promise I'd made two years before. With our belongings packed in the trunk of my car and with her father hanging onto my sideview mirror, I backed out of our driveway and left. He was devastated.

My daughter's father didn't fight me in court, so I gained full custody of her. He would have every-other-weekend visitations, which he kept until she was nine or ten years-old. Suddenly, without notice, he stopped meeting me for his weekend visits. His excuse was our daughter did not want to see him anymore. Whenever she was with him, she spent all her time with his sister and her husband.

My daughter is now twenty-two. We've lived a hard life together. She has been through Hell and back with me so-to-speak. The absence of her father in her life has had a devastating impact on her. But in His mercy and grace, God gave me a great sense of peace about my daughter's future and her secured salvation. I will explain later the vision God gave me in 2002 during the most difficult years with her. This vision was what I have relied upon all these years, as God knew exactly what I would need to see in order to have hope that she would be okay.

Chapter 12

Someone to Lean On

"Cast your burden on the Lord, and he will sustain you;
he will never allow the righteous to be shaken."
Psalm 55:22 CSB

I was twenty-one when Dad hit his ultimate bottom and waved the white flag. He joined Alcoholics Anonymous (AA) and later started a workout regimen that helped him to shed fifty pounds. At long last, a new emotion arose in my soul. Its name was *hope.*

Remember that I previously told you my two parents were extremely determined people. Well, Dad religiously followed the twelve-step program, which laid the foundation and groundwork for the best eight years of our lives together. He was ecstatic to learn of my pregnancy and was determined to be the best granddaddy ever. After my daughter was born, Dad loved to visit with her.

She was born during the Beanie Baby craze. My dad was determined to give her something she would be able to one day look back on and know it came from him. He began his search for the rarest and most valuable bears after learning the gender of his granddaughter. I would guess hundreds of hours went into his search as he visited flea markets, online retailers, and hobby stores almost daily before her birth. By the time she was born, she had 278 Beanie Babies, each in individual plastic containers. With a smile I say, "Now you see why I described Dad as having a rare chip of determination."

Thankfully, my father's sobriety shaped him into someone

I could lean on for the first time. God knew I would need him in the years ahead. Like Mom, when he made a commitment to something, he was all in and full steam ahead. Not only was he attending seven AA meetings per week, but he also became a well-known sponsor in his region.

When he passed away people from all over the world contacted me to let me know how much he had changed their lives or assisted them in some way. As previously mentioned, dad was a recluse. In the early 2000's he discovered a new technology called, "Web-TV." This was the ever so slow television internet platform that a used dial-up internet provider so the end user could surf the web while watching television. My dad loved to play sweepstakes. He was a trivia wiz, so the internet allowed him to connect with individuals across the globe who also competed in various sweepstakes contests. Little did I know that my dad had become the leading trivia expert for people all over the world needing answers. They would enter a prospective contest and receive a trivia question, which they would in-turn send to my dad for an answer. After winning the contest they would send him money or gifts. He had a global network right from the comfort of his living room.

Soon after his passing, I was contacted by various Alcohol Anonymous sponsees he had supported during his years of sobriety. Bo Pickler, father of country singer Kelly Pickler contacted me as well. He told me that my dad was the reason he was alive. During a time when he was at bottom and ready to die, my dad was used mightily by God to help him back to his feet, pick up a white chip, and enter the great world of alcohol freedom. Tears flowed down my cheeks as I would listen to the various reports and stories; I had no idea my father had been so influential in the lives of others. What a gift from God!

What I Experienced During My Visit with God

What you are going to read in this section was not a vision. It was as real as your reading this right now. *The 700 Club* mistakenly referred to what happened to me as a *vision,* but there were only a few visions during the visitation with God.

Chapter 13

The Voices

"But you are not like that, for you are a chosen people.
You are royal priests, a holy nation, God's very own
possession. As a result, you can show others the goodness
of God, for he called you out of the darkness into his
wonderful light. Once you had no identity as a people; now
you are God's people. Once you received no mercy; now
you have received God's mercy."
1 Peter 2: 9-10 NLT

In February of 2002, I began to hear voices in my head, and not the type they ask you about on psych exams. They were terrifying voices that gave subtle commands to me, starting softly and progressing to a higher volume and frequency. When I refused to listen to them, their frequency and volume became greater over time. Most of these voices uttered phrases I would never think or say.

Before this experience, I would have never believed this type of thing really occurred. I was desensitized by the Hollywood horror movies and my sin, so I didn't believe it was real. I was blinded by Satan more each day, and he was leading me right to the pit of Hell. The voices started getting louder and more frequent, even going so far as to say, "Kill your daughter." Of course, my daughter was my everything, so I knew these voices were evil.

As a child, I'd always fantasized about becoming a mother and desired the joy of giving a child all the love my heart could hold. I'd never do anything to harm her, but the

49

worst was still yet to come.

I tried to make the voices stop by cupping my ears, singing a song, or saying aloud, "Stop that!" or "Leave me alone!" Satan was cleverly using my vulnerability and my lack of Biblical knowledge to forever cut me off from meeting God. Now, I know he attempted to prevent me from fulfilling the divine purpose for which I was created. Although Satan does not know your future, as the believer's future is hidden in Christ, he certainly knows when God has appointed you for something special in His redemptive program for humanity.

Finally, a crescendo occurred the weekend before June 7, 2002. I had been planning a yard sale to earn extra money. My boyfriend had left for a job and would be gone until the following Monday, so the conditions were just right for this perfect demonic storm brewing inside my mind. The enemy knew isolation was the key to unhindered harassment, so the frequency and volume of the attacks increased. Having reached a dead end to all other attempted instruction, the voices then took one last ditch effort to drag me feet first into Hell. This time I heard, "Blaspheme the Holy Spirit," and although I did not know it was the one unpardonable sin, I knew not to listen. One thing is for certain: Never would I have thought to say something so diabolically wicked.

Until that moment, I thought perhaps I was going crazy. Though I would never act upon the instructions, the voices were trying to break me down little by little, making me believe I was insane. Instead of achieving their intention of invoking my eternal damnation, when I heard the reference to the Holy Spirit, I fully understood the pure evil that was invading my mind. But the question was *Who was the voice?* I was to learn Satan knew God was about to do something wonderful in my life. He didn't know what it was exactly, but he knew I was marked for God.

Satan sent his legions to attempt diversion and thwart my

regeneration. He knew many lives would be impacted with my testimony. From all the Hell Satan had led me through on earth up until this point, this was the pinnacle. I was his prisoner; my mind was held captive. I was in bondage where I knew nothing of God's power to extinguish the flames rising all around me. Unfortunately, I wasn't equipped to fight this demonic legion coming against me.

Chapter 14

June 7, 2002

"What sorrow for those who say that evil is good
and good is evil, that dark is light and light is dark,
that bitter is sweet and sweet is bitter."
Isaiah 5:20 NLT

During this time in my life, I was bartending at a local bar. My husband-to-be refused to punch a clock, so he traveled to and from his jobs, pressure washing. Sometimes, he would be gone for a few days. I hated being alone, especially at night. As explained earlier, childhood fear pervaded my life. Because my dad enjoyed watching horror films, I watched them with him until he passed out from drinking all evening. All night I laid in bed, afraid of the dark. This didn't change as a young adult. The drug my boyfriend and I were using eased my inhibitions, so I didn't experience the fear anymore. Staying alone while my boyfriend traveled wasn't so bad if the drug was available. But the voices had overridden all the false comfort I received by using the drug. I was terrified at that point to be alone.

My boyfriend, who will from this point forward be referred to as John, had to leave for a three-day trip. When he realized he wouldn't have enough of the drug to last him, he took what we had, leaving me with none to get by. I didn't realize the ramifications of abruptly discontinuing the drug, but I agreed he needed it more than I did. I took my last dose before going to bed that night.

Around 2:00 a.m. on June 7, 2002, I was awakened

rather slowly by an audible and angelic voice speaking softly in my ear. I was half-asleep, so it seemed like a dream, but I recognized the familiar voice, a voice so soothing and comforting. "Paige, Paige. Oh Paige, wake up dear. Wake up. Wake up and listen to me."

As I became more cognizant, I recognized the voice to be that of my future mother-in-law, the lady from whom I received such comfort and peace. At first, I was afraid, but then a sweeping feeling of peace came over me. Instead of the blaring, yet non-audible tormenting voices, this voice was audible and crystal clear. Oddly enough, I realized this was not her, but then, who was it? Vaguely, I tried to reconcile what was happening, so I responded.

"Yes, I am awake. Who is this?"

The reply was immediate: "Paige, don't be afraid. I woke you using this voice because I knew it would provide you with comfort due to the torment you have been experiencing. I didn't want to scare you. The voices you have been hearing, Paige, were from Satan. His goal was to get you to take your life and that of your family, but I am here to rescue you. However, I must show you some things first."

Explaining the events that followed will be hard for me to convey and futile, using the limited number of human words we have. I remember asking the voice how it knew to come to me? Instead of an audible answer, I saw a vision this time.

The vision was of my future father- and mother-in-law. These two devout Christians were in their bedroom, praying for me. Although my boyfriend and I had tried to justify our living together was to combine our expenses and save money, they were unhappy with our living arrangements. Instead of expressing their disdain for our sinful state, they went to the Lord with prayerful petitions, requesting His divine intervention. I interpreted this as concern about our future. They questioned if we were right for each other?

In the vision, I could see God heeding their requests and sending answers to their prayers. Something else stood out to me. They were acting as intercessors for me personally. Though the request was initially about our living arrangements, the Lord used it as an opportunity to completely regenerate me and show me I was chosen for His kingdom's purpose, and it was very distinguished. He wanted me to know I had a particular assignment on this earth.

This is when the voice began to change. No longer was it audible or the voice of my future mother-in-law. It transformed into a *still small voice*. The voice would respond to my thoughts before I could even fully articulate a sentence. What followed turned into a very unpleasant experience. The comforting and peaceful feeling I felt earlier was completely gone. It was replaced by fear. I had known fear throughout my life but not this fear. It was a Godly, reverent fear unlike anything I had ever faced. The atmosphere of the bedroom was empty -- like nothingness, dark and dank -- nothingness. It was as if I were entering into a holding place in my spirit. Then, one by one, childhood visions flashed before me. It was like seeing video recordings of my life, which were somewhere, anticipating my review. For example, when a plane crashes, the black box is retrieved – providing an audible story of what happened prior to the crash.

An even deeper sense of emptiness and nothingness washed over me. It was as if I were dead. Of course, it was still night, so the darkness of night made it all much worse. Though I was lying in bed, I was transported to a holding cell that was cold and damp. There was no way out. My mind was filled with *what I should have done differently during my life.* I instantly became all too aware of the time I had wasted. I thought of my family who would miss me, especially my precious daughter.

I was shown my parents partying and the sinful state in which I was conceived. I witnessed my childhood and the evil chasing me throughout life. My receding familial generations had allowed the demonic realm to enter my life through open doors. Not only had I been influenced by this generational iniquity, but I had also begun to participate in it. I had been bound by it as I grew from childhood into young adulthood.

Many people have said that at the point of death, you feel no pain. The pain will disappear, and at least the person will hurt no more. This is not true. The truth I would come to learn the hard way is that only in Christ will the individual not experience the pain of death. If one is not saved, he/she will not only feel the pain of death but also the pain of those whom they have harmed. Unfortunately, this has been the experience of so many who could have easily accepted the Way, the Truth, and the Life. I thought I was saved. I really did. I had prayed the sinner's prayer and recited the words. As a little girl, I was confirmed as a Lutheran. As a young adult, I was baptized as a Baptist. Neither of those *traditions* sealed my salvation as I later would learn. Unfortunately, this means there are many who might have a pew in church but not a place in Heaven.

What I was seeing was an examination of my life or what you might call a life review. Secret desires of my heart were revealed to me. I believed I was a *good person* but didn't comprehend what *good* truly meant in its *spiritual* sense. I saw the innate wickedness of the human heart, especially mine. Lies I had told throughout my life came to mind.

I had lied to everyone by painting a faux reality that was separate and apart from the abuse I had experienced as a child and young adult. I lied about my father because I was ashamed of who he had become and the filth in which he lived and accepted as normal. Whenever I lied, I would think, *It was only a white lie or a little lie, so it wasn't that bad.* But I had only fooled myself. A lie is a lie, period! Yes, even I began to believe my own lies and continued to repeat them as if they were the truth, that is, until the moment when God said, "No more!" Honestly, I was unaware or had forgotten most of what was being brought before me. In complete adoration, I knew God was speaking to me. No one or nothing else could explain it away.

My visions were lightning fast. When one thinks of having a vision, various things come to mind. A vision could be many things. One could have a vision of their daily tasks or a vision in the night or early morning. The only reason I use the word *vision* here is because I have nothing else with which to relate. It was more like a telepathic tape God was showing me. As one tape would finish, the next one would start. There were certain parts of the tape I wanted to stop or rewind- hit pause- or play again. I could do that as God had provided the reel and remote. The party scenes with my boyfriend and me were clearly visible. I saw a summation of sins in which I was willingly involved and in agreement, which was accounted to me. There were many sins accounted to me. When this part of my review was completed, I felt such a burden of condemnation and no sense of relief in knowing I had a Savior. There was no release in knowing my Savior understood because I had been such a victim of circumstance. Although I could logically understand why those sins were not that bad, it did not matter. I learned *sin* is *sin.*

Chapter 15

Highway to Hell

"Enter by the narrow gate; for wide is the gate
and broad is the road that leads to destruction,
and many enter through it. But small is the gate and narrow
the road that leads to life, and only a few find it."
Matthew 7:13-14 NIV

After judging my life and showing me the wrong I'd committed, once again a strange emptiness overwhelmed me as if I were dead. Within a few minutes, I was returned to the cold and damp holding cell with no way out. The hard concrete floor served as a metaphor for the stone heart I had for so long. Once again, I could only think about what I should have done differently in my life, the time I had wasted, and my grieving family, especially my precious daughter.

It didn't seem as if I were restrained in the cell long before I was back in my bed, but no one was asleep beside me. Remember, John was out of town, but I had entered what seemed like another dimension. Whether in my body or out, I do not know. But I was not in my day-to-day reality at this point. If there is something to which I may compare, it was like the movie, *The Matrix*.

As I walked down the hall to the living room, the concept of eternity became noticeably clear. Wherever this was leading, I knew there was no way out. The atmosphere was thick, dim, and cold, a penetrating cold I felt in my bones. My breathing was labored with the overwhelming fear that clinched my throat. There was a weird smell – like death and formaldehyde. No life, no oxygen, no sense of anything but death and decay existed. I remember the shriveled, pruning feel of my skin. It was as if I'd been dead and decaying for years. I knew I was in big trouble but thought certainly it would be over soon. I felt the chilly darkness here, as well. There are no words to express the fear I felt.

The thoughts of squandering so many opportunities and being here forever sent shudders down my spine. In addition, time didn't exist – only the realization of eternity.

My memories include horrifying screams in the distance, the type of screams that are fueled with dread and hopelessness. The painful moaning of the lost souls echoed throughout the rooms of our house. Blindly, I searched room after room, quickly becoming aware there was no turning back and no chance of repentance.

My comprehension of *eternity* became distinct as my carnal mind could never quite grasp it before. After rounding the corner into the den, I was relieved to see John lying on the couch, face down, which was odd. The closer I moved toward him, the more he began to move. I said, "Why are you face down on the couch?"

When he turned to face me, terror struck my body like a lightning bolt; his face was pitted, hollowed, and his eyes were black, even though in life they were crystal blue. He was dirty, and he looked like someone does after death in a morgue but with baggy filthy clothes on his decrepit body. With untold terror streaking down my spine, it was as if he were possessed by a demon or worse, he was a demon and not my boyfriend at all. Then he spoke and cried loudly, "Why did you have to die? What am I going to tell your daughter?"

I asked, "What do you mean? I'm right here. I'm fine." But as I spoke, he never stopped crying and acknowledged me. He walked in circles, repeating the same sentences over and over. When I attempted to touch him, my hand passed through him. That's when I cried out, "Oh my Lord? No, please, no! What have I done?" Shaking in fear and not knowing if he was going to attack, I slowly backed away only to watch him return to the couch to resume the same face-down position.

Wait! This had to be a dream. With a big gulp, I silently crept toward him again. It was when I got within a few steps, he was triggered. At once he stood, turned to face me, and repeated once again, "Why did you have to die? What am I going to tell your daughter?" Suddenly it was clear -- he was a demon programmed to activate when I neared him. That was the moment I knew -- I WAS IN HELL!

With this realization came one more: I couldn't hear what I was saying. The words were in my thoughts with no audible sound whatsoever. Each time I tried to speak to John, the same scene was repeated. Then, I heard the television click on automatically without pressing a button. I quickly reached for the remote to lower the volume but discovering nothing but the channels could be changed. There were only two stations available on the cable box. On the first station, an evangelist preached the Word of God and the message of salvation. On the second channel, I saw many people turning from the Lord and mocking the cross. It was clear that I had lived for myself and not for Christ, so I began to cry. But I found I had zero ability to express emotion. This inability was a miserable feeling in the midst of all these surfacing sensations. My senses were heightened, more so than ever before in my life. This couldn't be real, so I had to escape. I headed toward the front door.

We lived on a beautiful lake with an incredible view. I was able to see outside, so I reasoned, *If I could get outside, then this will end, and I can change my life before it's too late.* When I opened the sliding glass door, I gasped from the intense heat of the outdoors. As soon as I began to turn the lock, I was zapped with a jolt of electricity that seemed like a stun gun. When I stubbornly returned to try it once more, the jolt sensation was stronger. I felt it penetrate my entire body. The stifling heat prevented me from filling my lungs with oxygen. Oxygen, but wait -- there wasn't any oxygen.

I could walk freely about the house, so I ventured into my daughter's room. As I noticed the photos and memories surrounding me, I could only wish I would have lived for the Lord and not myself. I longed to just hold my daughter again, and whisper, "Mommy is going to be okay." Instead, I heard cries from those who missed me. My daughter would grow up without a Mommy; instantly the pain she would feel became my pain at that moment. The pain was on a much more magnified level; it ripped me apart.

Deep within my soul, I knew what had happened to me. Reality was becoming clearer as I once again discerned there was no way out of this place. I couldn't scream, cry, or beg for help. The most horrific thing was I knew I was lost in Hell. All I did from that moment on was walk around, looking at photos that brought back memories, wishing I could have lived for the Lord. I also saw my daughter without a mommy, and the pain was so great, I just wanted to die. Yet, I already was dead. I not only felt my pain, I felt the pain of loved ones, and that is what ripped me to shreds.

During funerals, people are heard to say, "At least they are no longer in pain." I can tell you this: If you have not given your life to the Lord, you will feel your pain and the pain of everyone you have ever harmed in your entire life. This will never stop; it will last for eternity. Unfortunately, this was it for me. As I looked around me, I saw the sin in my life and the times I had turned from the Lord. I had nothing else to do except think! All the fleshly pursuits of sin, including vanity and sensuality, were turned upside down and thrown back at me.

My thoughts progressed to eternity. *If I am going to be in this place for eternity, what will happen next month, next year, and the years that follow?* Then I was shown the walls decaying with webbing and spiders everywhere. This would be it. The Hell I had made on earth would be the Hell I would live in for eternity. Exhausted and with no hope for a reprieve, I laid down on the couch in our front living room.

I still couldn't speak or cry; nothing was working. I closed my eyes and could picture tears inside. I was screaming inside, begging God to give me another chance. As I opened my eyes, they were blurred by real tears, which were streaming onto my cheeks and onto my throat. My pleas to God were those out-of-control, gut-wrenching sobs, which you cry during the saddest moments or outbursts of pain and anguish.

Then, I saw them.

Chapter 16

The Fear of Reverence

"In his kindness God called you to share in his eternal glory by means of Christ Jesus. So, after you have suffered a little while, he will restore, support, and strengthen you, and he will place you on a firm foundation."
1 Peter 5:10 NLT

Suddenly, I was terrified when I saw the outline of two men standing over me. *What now?* I asked myself. When the tears cleared, I recognized John and his best friend standing in the same front living room where I was. I had returned to the physical realm; I was back in real time.

John was crying, begging me to snap out of it. His friend asked, "What do you think is happening to her?" to which he responded, "She is losing her mind or having a nervous breakdown of some sort." Once I got myself peeled off the couch, I began hugging both of them like a maniac coming out of a coma. Finally, I found my voice as I screamed aloud, "It's over, and I am free! Thank God, I am free from Hell!"

It is extremely difficult to explain the anguish I felt during my seemingly long, but realistically short separation from God. Somehow, I knew this experience was only a foretaste of what would await me if major lifestyle changes did not occur. Not that I doubted Hell was a real place, but for me it was a lack of understanding. I had heard many of those Southern Baptist hellfire, and brimstone messages preached over the years, but now I have an impression imprinted of its stark reality that will last forever.

It is impossible to convey the untold pure terror that I felt and would have felt for eternity if I had died in my sins. Then God showed me that the Hell I experienced was the lesser of the two damnations. Oh, yes! There is a greater, much more severe punishment! As terrifying as my experience was, it was nothing compared to the further depths of punishment, which many will experience. I knew I had been in Hell, but how in the world was anyone going to believe me? Only God and I knew at that moment what I had experienced. It became obvious to me that millions of people are clueless about the other side. Judgment is going to happen, and all those who have mocked the Lord and have bathed in their sin and not accepted the truth will never have the opportunity again after they step into eternity.

As I felt an urgency to tell others, the Lord said, "For an appointed time." After the full realization of my experience set in, God retracted my sense of terror and replaced it with a sense of peace, like switching off a light switch. Not that the memory had been removed, or it could not surface again, I knew it was stored away for now. Just like everything else the Lord taught me; I knew that feeling could surface again.

I was not tuned into a panoramic view of my separation from God. It wasn't a trance like Peter experienced when envisioning the sheet let down from Heaven in Acts, chapter 10. Perhaps a trance is more comparable to watching a movie with surround sound. It most certainly was not an out-of-body experience as some others have described in their supernatural revelations of Hell.

Regarding the Apostle Paul's visit to the third Heaven, he said, "I was caught up to the third Heaven fourteen years ago. Whether I was in my body or out of my body, I don't know—only God knows" (2 Corinthians 12:2, NLT). I know what I experienced was real.

If I had to parallel a Biblical account, I would liken it

to Phillip being carried away by the Spirit of the Lord after sharing the good news about Jesus to the eunuch. I was transported to this place of death and decay, a place that truly defined separation from the Godhead. I have believed for many years that my experience was only shown to me, so I could be forewarned about what would have happened to me if my death had occurred at that time in my life. With all five senses in operation (except tears, although crying and wailing internally), my experience was as life like as you, the reader, touching this book or electronic device while reading my story with your full faculties present.

Jesus said there was a greater and a lesser damnation (Matthew 23:14). I do not want either one! Praise God for His sacrifice! Praise God we have a Savior who restored our ability to be in full relationship with the Trinity: Father, Son, and Holy Ghost.

In Scripture, Jesus mentioned *Hell* many more times than He mentioned *Heaven*. It is vital to understand why judgement exists and why Jesus warned us about it so many times. His love for us wants the best for us, which is why He suffered so much on the cross for sin. The judgement we deserve was laid upon Him, as an atoning sacrifice for the punishment we deserve. I never fully understood this until His visit with me and the vision of where my life was headed without the cross.

Chapter 17

Connecting the Points

"All Scripture is God-breathed and is useful for teaching,
rebuking, correcting and training in righteousness,
so that the servant of God may be thoroughly
equipped for every good work"
2 Timothy 3:16-17 NIV

I thought I was a bad person, and the past was all my fault. God showed me that I although I was accountable for my sin, there was much I didn't know and could not have known had He not shown me the unseen details about my early life. He allowed me to see videos of my life as a child. It was like a video camera was on the wall always recording no matter where I was. The Lord showed me how and when the abuse began, as early as three years old. In one scene I saw that my fourth stepdad, the one who enslaved me as his personal prostitute in our home, would visit my room while I was asleep. He would slip his hand under the covers and fondle me prior to me knowing he was there. This is just one of many examples of how the enemy groomed me year after year through various individuals. This preparation was a setup for my ultimate surrender to his evil whiles and ways. As I matured, so did my captivity to sinful patterns.

Living a lie was normal to me. Beginning with my stepbrother's molestation and subsequent sexual enslavement by my stepdad, secrets meant survival. Even though I lived a dual life as a child and was taught lying was what I had to do, during this part of God's visitation, I was shown how the abuse opened the door to subsequent sin. I was reminded of lies that I had fabricated as a child to paint a picture, far from the reality of the abuse. I remembered the lies I had told to make myself appear socially acceptable because I lacked identity and self-worth. Lying had become a part of my everyday life. I lied to myself just as much as I lied to others. I even began to believe my own lies and continued to repeat them as if they were truth until that very moment when God commanded, "No more!"

I had never fully understood the fear of God until that night, but I will never forget it as long as I live. It is forever enshrined in my heart.

Just then a shift occurred. I went from the visions of sin patterns to my eyes being zeroed in on a bottle containing our drug of choice inside the bathroom cabinet, which was visible from our bed. It suddenly hit me! I had a vivid realization of how the sin patterns led to enslavement by the spirit of addiction, then God said, "This will be your last dose. Get up and take one half of what you normally consume. Close the lid and place it back in a secret location, so your daughter won't be able to locate it."

God illustrated the severity of the withdrawal I would have faced had He not interceded. I laid back in the bed and realized this was not a dream. The Creator of the Universe was speaking directly to me. I knew this was different than the voices of the enemy I'd heard before. I feared God, but it was more a reverent, respectful type of fear, not one of terror. His presence was clear, and I knew I was either in trouble or dying because I had not been doing the right thing. Explaining the hours that followed that night are difficult due to the depth and width of things I was shown.

Although I had been awake all night, when morning came, I felt rested. It was divine rest. I would experience this same "rest" throughout the remainder of His visit. Little did I know that I couldn't sleep because the power of God was so strong, therefore sleep was not an option. But the divine rest is something that I will never forget. That next morning, my boyfriend left for his job, but he knew something wasn't quite right with me.

Throughout the day I recognized I was in the beginning stages of withdrawal, but I never felt anything. God protected me from it all. Off and on throughout the day, God showed me behavior issues I never realized were present in my daily routine. I was affected by my childhood more than I could ever have imagined.

Months prior to God's visit, I'd won a *Playboy Magazine* contest, which included a four-day, all expenses paid trip to the Playboy Mansion in California. This was hard to refuse, so I left on my trip. While there, my behavior was less than desired, especially at a *Playboy* party, when I got high. Honestly, it was like I was out of my mind and made one poor decision after another while I was there. One terrible decision was that I cheated on my boyfriend. And there was no excuse for my actions. In response, God told me, "You must confess this to him, along with the sexual abuse."

Before I returned home from the trip, I met a key person who was the manager for *Playboy* centerfolds for each month of the calendar. He gave me his card and asked if I would be interested in a photo shoot. It was an easy $100 K for selling my soul to the devil.

That's when God warned, "Don't do this." Immediately, I felt convicted for even entertaining the idea. I never realized all the fleshly avenues the enemy will open up to us just to distract us from becoming the child God always wanted us to be. I knew I didn't belong in this environment. As flattering as it was for all the wrong reasons, I knew this was not the path the Lord had for me. After realizing the ugliness of this industry, I left my *Playboy* experience and the $100 K behind along with the lion's den from which God had saved me.

God showed me the dangers of toxins in the body. To this day, I do not understand the significance of some of the specifics, but I intend on asking Him when I get to Heaven. There were many other warnings and visions regarding my behavior, which are too detailed to breakdown now.

God literally showed me the pollution in my body after a night of partying on the lake. We had a 28-foot long cruiser that we used as our party boat. My boyfriend and I were invited to double date with another couple on the weekend during God's visit. God showed me there would be drugs on the boat. He allowed us to go out with them in order to teach further lessons. Of course, I thought, *After a visit from God, I will never touch drugs again,* but let us just say God had a different plan in mind. When the drugs surfaced, God said, "Go ahead." No matter how much of the drug I consumed, I could not get high. I felt nothing and was clueless as to why this was allowed.

God began to show me the reality of what other people looked like while high, and the sexual perversion I had been a part of before. But now, I was fully sober. It played out before me like a horrifying documentary. The entire scene was depraved, self-centered, pleasure-oriented, and a clear path to destruction. These are the same people I had built my life around, and it sickened my spirit to see my reflection looking back at me. Usually, coming down from the high was the worst part for me as it made me feel so bad, I just wanted to die. It was painful, and I would cry and promise myself, "I will never do this again."

Since I learned so much while we were out with the other couple, I thought the lesson was over. Little did I know it was just the beginning of a long night of instruction from the Lord. After John went to sleep, I felt a tug on my hand. God led me to the mirror in our master bathroom. Suddenly, my body experienced the high from the night before on the lake. I immediately felt the destruction in my body, the toxicity in my tissues, and the pain of coming down from cocaine. I felt like a trash dump full of garbage.

We do not realize these things because they come about slowly as we are getting high, regardless of the substance. The mind is being altered while the drug is destroying our cells, resulting in a false sense of feeling good. Fortunately, I was never a good partier because I hated the feeling. After my visit with God, no one on the lake liked to party with me after the first few hours because I began to preach to them. Yes, I was a great hypocrite!

God placed visions in my mind of people I had wronged, their feelings, and even their hatred of me. It was not all bad though because the Lord showed me that He knew I did not want to do what I was doing. He knew all my inner conflicts, even ones I could not identify. Once I realized the full extent of the Lord's reason for allowing this to manifest, He showed me what my skin would look like in the future if I kept abusing my body in this way. Oh, I had no idea how much damage I was doing to myself until the visions of self-destruction. Although I was not a smoker, I smoked while I was high, pack after pack; it was disgusting!

Then the tables turned to the internal, self-inflicted destruction that had manifested in me over the years. Due to my inner poison from all the secrets, I began to purge after each meal as a release. God said, "You must stop, or you will die." I was committing internal suicide and did not even realize it. He revealed areas in my life where I was causing conflict, not doing the right thing, or simply small revelations that would make a big difference if implemented.

After the bad came the good. After the discipline came love and tenderness. Like parents disciplining their children, God did not stop loving me because of my sin. It was just the opposite. Because of His love for me, my Father disciplined me. I recognized this love was unlike anything I had ever felt in my life.

As all these thoughts fully registered, I returned to the mirror to discover my reflection had changed. My face was beautiful, radiant, and glowing like I had never seen it before. It looked like light beams were shooting through my pores. I had always struggled with five pounds here or there, but suddenly, my waist had shrunk to a size that was the desire of my heart. My right eye winked once, followed by a chime. Telepathically, I knew God was showing me that at some point, this would happen. This winking had happened many times with a single blink on the right for yes and double blink on the left meaning no, followed by a chime. It was strange that I just knew what He meant without words.

Then God led me to my daughter's bedroom where she was peacefully sleeping. Instantly, I felt this overwhelming love down deep into the pit of my spirit. God showed me the level of love in my heart for her. He said, "I know that you love her, but you have put her above me." I was immediately convicted of this and asked for His forgiveness. As I looked out of the corner of my eye, I saw the shadow of a spirit descending upon her. I knew in my heart it was the Holy Spirit. The Lord confirmed my thoughts and gave me assurance He would protect and keep her. I felt so undeserving of this gratuitous love and could not imagine ever disappointing Him again.

Chapter 18

Heaven or Nothing

"My Father's house has many rooms;
if that were not so, would I have told you that I am
going there to prepare a place for you?
And if I go and prepare a place for you,
I will come back and take you to be with me
that you also may be where I am."
John 14: 2-3 NLT

As I was lying in bed, I thought about the profound experiences I'd been privy to throughout the week when I was removed from reality and taken to a special place of peace. It was as if I were traveling through the blackness of space, yet it was warm and serene. Off in the far distance, I saw a speck of light. It seemed as if I was being pulled toward it, but I didn't know why. As I drew closer to the light, I experienced feelings of utter peace, tranquility, and contentment. Imagine those feelings multiplied by a thousand times. Then they filled every pore of my body. These emotions of joy, peace, love, and serenity completely enveloped me.

As I moved closer to the light, it was spectacular, more so than I could begin to describe. I've never seen or could imagine anything like it. It was and still is the most remarkable sight I've ever seen to this day. I won't even attempt to string enough adjectives back-to-back-to-back to describe the beauty before me. It is futile to believe I'll ever have the words to give it justice. Even the great artist, Michelangelo, and the marvelous splendor of the Sistine Chapel's ceilings couldn't begin to capture the beauty and majesty of this light. It was indescribable because of a feeling associated with the light. Think of your fondest memory and the best feeling you've ever had. Multiply by several billion. That's the only fitting description I can derive.

This brilliant light grew brighter and larger the closer I got to it. Could this be the entrance to heaven, I asked myself? Wherever I was, I never wanted to leave. Although I had a beloved three-year-old daughter whom I adored, and a family, all I wanted was to remain in this brilliant light. I realized there was no sense of time as there had been in Hell. The joy inside was so real and immense, my senses were heightened beyond any sense experienced on earth. There was no pain, fear, or anxiety – only liquid love! Once I could comprehend this, I simultaneously felt my right eye wink and heard a chime. I knew God was confirming what I was thinking about the light.

I understood God's communication without using words; it was as if we were 'thinking' sentences to each other. Even though I tried hard to see God, I couldn't see anything beyond the light. For a moment imagine a light thousands of times larger than the sun and brighter than any burst of brilliant white light; a light so bright it blinded the Apostle Paul while on the Road to Damascus. That light was what I saw however, instead of blinding me, it enveloped me. Envision a light with the power to create the entire universe in a split second. That is a fitting description of what I experienced. Others have testified to the light, now I have not only seen it, but I have also journeyed far, far into it.

The Lord showed me people who had gone before me. They were in a place, which couldn't be explained but I knew they were there until an appointed time. At some point, we will all travel away from this earth to be eternally with God or not. My hope is that if you are reading this book right now, you will yearn to know Christ as Savior and never look back again. He is real, He is perfection. Although I never entered "the gates of heaven" so-to-speak, the Lord confirmed the reality of it to me in His own way. It's difficult to explain how He placed thoughts and meanings into my mind, but He did.

When I opened my eyes, I saw the four walls of my bedroom. John was asleep beside me. It was as if he didn't have a care in the world. He was oblivious to what had just happened to me.

After that night, I've longed to experience the magnificence of those moments again. My heart is assured this is a snippet of what I can anticipate when I go home to be with our Lord.

Chapter 19

The Good News

"The gatekeeper opens the gate for him,
and the sheep recognize his voice and come to him.
He calls his own sheep by name and leads them out.
After he has gathered his own flock, he walks ahead of
them, and they follow him because they know his voice."
John 10: 3-4 NLT

Immediately after my visit into the light and Hell, I was given a short reprieve. Wait! What had just happened to me? If you can imagine shock in the gravest sense of the word, then that is the shock I experienced during my short break. Therefore, it was impossible to think about anything other than what had occurred. It was impossible to go about normal activities. As the day progressed, I attempted to digest what I'd been shown using subjectivity and objectivity. I was angry. I was sad. And I was hopeful that He would return, even if it meant being shown what could be painful.

While I was wrought with reverent fear of God, I also longed for that daily dosage of deep communication to continue. Is it possible, Dear Lord? Can our communication be so fluid, vivid, and intense with you? Never had I considered whether it was possible to connect so deeply, so intimately with the Lord God himself. Sure enough, the respite was fleeting.

That night instead of hearing His voice, I felt a tug on my hand. At first, I was fearful, but excitement overwhelmed me. When the first tug wasn't acknowledged, another one quickly followed. I couldn't see anyone in the room, yet I tried to ignore what I felt. *Surely, this cannot be real. Am I going to revisit Hell again?* I thought. I resisted several times, testing what I was feeling, proving to myself that I wasn't sleepwalking, and ensuring I wasn't imagining this. Even though I tried to stall, the tug became stronger, more urgent. I certainly didn't want to rock the boat, so I slowly moved out of the bed, heeding His request. Then I asked, "What is next, Lord?"

From this night forward, whenever the Lord awakened me, it was with a gentle, yet pronounced tug on my hand – like an invisible squeeze. One night in particular, the Lord led me down the stairs of our house to the basement. As I walked from place to place, He revealed visions of my spiritual carelessness. Then He shared what I needed to do for protection from future invasions of the enemy into my life.

God used the door leading from the basement to the outside to illustrate how the enemy crouches at the door, waiting for the opportune time to attack. This was followed by another vision of an attempted break-in at this door. Mesmerized, I watched the scene flash before me. Incredibly, my boyfriend and I had been alerted out of a deep sleep one night when someone tried to break the glass in that door. My boyfriend hurried out of bed to turn on the lights. In a matter of seconds, we watched the would-be-thief run across the yard, disappearing into the darkness. Gratefully, the door was locked, so the attempt had been unsuccessful. The Lord told me I'd been careless and reminded me how important it was to do my part. Then He could more easily do His part.

Years later during another visitation, the Lord explained this regarding spiritual carelessness. "The Shepherd is always with you and has the best in mind for you, but you must keep your boundaries. If not, He will not be able to keep His."

I'm reminded of the conversation Kevin Costner had with Whitney Houston in the movie, *The Bodyguard.* It really stuck with me because it is an exact correlation to the Lord's message about carelessness. Houston was playing the role of a famous singer who had a crazy psycho stalking her. Costner was hired as her bodyguard. Without his knowledge or protection, she appeared at a local nightclub to debut a new song from her album. Crowd madness ensued while she was on stage, and Houston was injured. Afterward, Costner said, "I cannot protect you like this." What he meant was if you are not going to keep the boundaries per our agreement, I cannot keep mine.

Next, I was led to the upstairs sliding glass patio doors, which led outside to our in-ground pool. My daughter was three years old, but the Lord wasn't happy I'd carelessly left the patio doors unlocked during the day when I was home. I hadn't realized she was able to slide the doors open. Indeed, the Lord said it was unsafe and an access point for the enemy to hurt my family. He had me flip on the light and count the steps to the pool. There were only ten steps between the door and the pool. If you took the eleventh step, you landed in the water. The doors must be locked to ensure her safety was a top priority. Later, I would learn the significance of locking your doors spiritually, as well as physically.

In the years following that visitation, the Lord has revealed much of the spiritual significance I could not grasp at the time.

I have come to learn God doesn't waste anything. At that time, to me spiritual warfare was just something mythical like a *Marvel comic* book about how an evil creature had come to earth to defeat the world. As a former Baptist and subsequently a Lutheran, spiritual warfare was not familiar to me. I certainly didn't know what it was, but in God's vast wisdom, He knew I'd need this understanding later in our journey. It wasn't that God was not concerned about my daughter falling into the pool; He used it as a teaching tool. His greater message to me was how the enemy sneaks in our *back door* when we least expect him. He never knocks on the front door, alerting us to his presence, wiles, and ways. No, he uses the unsealed entrances. He uses the openings which we haven't guarded properly.

At the same time, I was being shown much about unresolved generational sin the bible refers to as iniquity. Iniquity passes from one generation to the next if not renounced, repented of, and put under the blood of Jesus. These sin patterns will be used by the enemy to create a hold on the next generation. The Lord was showing me that I must eliminate these entrances of evil, so they are not passed to my daughter.

Generational iniquities are tendencies, habits, or behavioral patterns we pick up from our parents or family members. Simple examples include a toxic thought life or constantly complaining. More deviant examples include murder or sorcery. If the curse isn't broken through the blood of Christ, the enemy will use this to develop a stronghold in the mind of his next targeted family victim.

Eventually, after nurturing the thoughts long enough, the individual will yield to the temptation, which results in a demonic demonization. An example of this would be a mother's demons that eventually are passed along to her daughter. But only after the daughter invites them in by opening the door to the sin. God does say He judges each one of us according to our own sin, not the sins of others because curses cannot land where they are not deserved. "As birds and sparrows fly, so a curse shall not come upon anyone without a cause" (Proverbs 26: 2, NIV).

Truly, I have experienced *coming under a curse* due to personal sin allowing the "bird to light" as mentioned in the scripture from Provers 26:2. Do not open yourself up to the schemes of the devil, but if you do, renounce that legal right you gave the enemy. This does not mean your salvation is lost. What it means is that your journey will be a lot more difficult as you are not fully repenting and closing that opened door to sin. Again, if not addressed, the generational demons will harass the offspring until they are persuaded into committing that same sin. Then the individual is in fact guilty, not because their ancestor is guilty. It's because now they, too, are guilty of committing the sin.

Jesus Christ frees us from these bondages and brings us into Himself for us to become more like Him in every way. Ask Him today if there are any open doors for the enemy to occupy space in your mind. How amazing is our God? I am forever grateful that He used such creative and unique ways to explain what was already in His Word. At this point in my life, I was beginning to understand the deep love Christ had for me.

The visitation went on for over a week, day, and night. During the daylight hours, I was placed in many scenarios with individuals, so the Lord could show me visions and speak words of knowledge, wisdom, and prophecy to them. Although I was in my present reality, the Lord would speak to me about each person. I would see visions of their lives and visions of their hearts for the Lord or lack thereof.

Depending on the situation for one of the individuals, the Lord often gave me a message (word of knowledge or word of encouragement) for them. Not all the messages I was given to speak to others were soothing. Sometimes I would have to tell the individual something I didn't necessarily want to say regarding personal sin in their lives. The message may be a warning of impending darkness. In each situation, the Lord specifically gave me the words to repeat.

Never in my life had I seen such powerful happenings,

especially coming from me. In my own opinion, I was the epitome of Paul's revelation to the Corinthians. "God chose the foolish things of the world to confound the wise; God chose the weak things of the world to shame the strong" (1 Corinthians 1:27, NIV).

Chapter 20

Rewiring with Love

"A cheerful heart is good medicine,
but a crushed spirit dries up the bones."
Proverbs 17:22 NIV

Man is made in God's image, but I have never pictured God having a sense of humor. He began to rewind the tape of my life again, highlighting many areas where the manipulation, abuse, and neglect began. This was not what He desired for me. Yes, I had to experience Hell, but it was His grace that allowed me to exit and start over. His grace is abundant and available for us all if we submit to His will.

Just for a moment, picture the thousands of veins running throughout your body. Then convert the veins to electrical wires that connect to a main switchboard in your back. A panel covers this switchboard, and a screw is tightly securing it in place on all four corners. This is important for you to understand the next vision. The Lord gave me one that really showed His sense of humor and His abundant grace. The vision showed the damage the enemy, through various people throughout my life had done to me. This resulted in my destructive behavior and emotions. I was a result of my environment.

Once all had registered, I began to hear noises, loud clanging, banging, and tapping. My attention was directed over my shoulder. As I peered over, I could not believe what was before my eyes. It was a small man dressed in an elf costume with a hat, shoes, and grey hair. He was whistling and singing as if He did not have a care in the world. I heard a drill unfasten each of the four screws that held the panel in place followed by clicking, hammering, and clanging sounds. He would say things like, "Oh, that doesn't belong there" or "My, we must reconnect this." It took Him a while, which meant I was really messed up, I guess. Finally, the elf was pleased with His work. I heard the four screws, one by one, being drilled back into position. It was funny because after He finished, I heard the winning sound from a game show -- ding, ding. Then He looked at me and winked. I knew exactly what had happened. I had been *rewired.* I erroneously thought the change would manifest at that moment and not over the next nine years.

Have you ever watched a game show or competition that included an applause meter? The applause meter indicates the power of that audience's inner conviction or their approval. Basically, the meter confirms if the one to whom the applause is given is liked or what they have said was either funny or compelling. Following the vision of being rewired, the Lord asked me, "Paige, do you love Me?" I thought that was quite strange for Him to ask and keep in mind that I didn't know the scriptures at that point in my life. Jesus had asked Peter just as He was asking me if I loved Him. I had only experienced God through religious practice, so an actual deeply rooted spring of love within my heart did not truly exist. But what was I going to say?

After experiencing Hell, I had a fear of God and a deep reverence; responding with anything other than yes was not an option. Therefore, Immediately I responded, "Yes Lord, I do love you." Suddenly I saw a vision of what looked to be a giant applause meter. Following my answer, I watched the needle on the applause meter barely move. It was like a lie detector test but illustrated by an applause meter instead. This was not the response I wanted to see. To my chagrin

I was asked a second time, "Paige, do you love Me?" And again, I said, "Yes, Lord I do love you," but this time I said it with more emphasis and inflection. My added passion would hopefully cause the meter to spring higher this time- but it didn't. Instead, the meter repeated the same little peak with maybe another bar or two added. This response was far from what I had expected. What was I to do? Just then I was asked a third time, "Paige, do you love Me?" This time I thought before I responded. If I am being asked once more, I thought, then He is probably upset with me. After a long pause I finally responded, "Lord, I want to love You." Without delay I saw the needle on the applause meter spring across the half-moon circle and ring a loud bell confirming it could go no further. Wow! All He wanted was my desire to love Him. How wonderful is our God! He gives us His spirit. The Holy Spirit not only causes us to walk in God's ways but also causes us to love Him (Ezekiel 36:27, Philippians 2:13, Deuteronomy 30:6). My right eye winked and I knew He was smiling at my humility and truthful response.

As with many other things God did during this visitation, I would later learn it was not the first time. Scripture confirmed He did them with others as well. I thank Him regularly for confirmations as I recall these stories.

Chapter 21

Releasing the Trauma

"Confess your sins to each other and pray for each other
so that you might be healed. The earnest prayer of the
righteous person has great power and
produces wonderful results."
James 5:16 NLT

Without confirmation from the Lord, I immediately blurted, "I'm having a visit from God" to John. Instead of sharing my joy, he frantically called my mother and asked her to find out what was wrong with me. He told her my behavior was alarming, and he was concerned about me. Mom had relocated to South Carolina after remarrying for the sixth time. She lived two hours from us but was on the scene shortly after their talk. At the time, I referred to her as a Narcotics Anonymous Nazi with no regard for Jesus or the Gospel. If any talk of God went outside the Higher Power she believed in, she would shut me down. Little did I know, God had a surprise for both of us. There were life impacting revelations about to develop.

At this point, I was far into my visit with God. Day and night it continued with only that one short reprieve. The Lord was speaking and showing me visions of my past, present, and future. I had no indication of my mother's intention. Mom had arrived in North Carolina to be with me; but things were about to take a drastic turn.

You see, Mom thought I had a great childhood and could not understand the poor choices I had made thus far in life.

When I heard her discussing my situation with John, I heard the Lord say, "You must confess the abuse of your childhood to your mother."

I immediately begged God not to make me do it. I felt ultimate fear shooting throughout every nerve ending in my body. *Why after all these years do I have to humiliate myself? What good will possibly come of this confession? Why are You punishing me?* God is a God of justice and allows the wrongs to be made right. This has been one of the most wonderful revelations to me about our Lord because He certainly straightens the crooked places in one's life. He did not have to answer my questions, but He chose to do so anyway.

For my relationship with my mother to be reconciled, God said, "We must start here." Then the Almighty showed me the true feelings in her heart for me. In her eyes, I was rebellious, without a premise for my actions. However, don't get me wrong. The Lord was not condoning the lies I told and my behavior, but He understood the choices I had made, resulting from years of abuse. My childhood had been completely robbed from me. Mom had no idea what was going on under her nose. After all the years of holding this inside, God said, "You must let it go." I attempted one last request to avoid this confession, but God's response was, "Where is your faith?" I kept hearing, "It all comes down to faith Paige!"

My mother was on the patio by the pool. I am sure she was wondering what in the world was going on with me. At that point, I had not told her I was being visited by the Creator of the Universe. As I sat, I heard God say, "Don't try to skip details. Just trust me."

I blatantly said, "Mom, I am having a visit from God. He's instructed me to tell you about something that happened a long time ago." As I began, I caught myself backing off out of fear, but it did not matter. I realized I had no control over my speech. The words began to flow regardless of my attempt to stop them. The sad part is, I had not planned on revealing details as I felt they weren't necessary, so I tried to curve the truth, but it was impossible. It was clear who was in the driver's seat; it certainly was not me.

"When I speak to you, I will open your mouth and shall say to them, this is what the Lord says" (Ezekiel 3:27, NIV). I dreaded sharing the intimate details of my life: the sexual abuse, the fear, the devastation of my life, and the mask I wore so brilliantly for all those years that had fooled her.

Then, I began to talk to her about religion, but God corrected me saying, "You have no right to do this now." For years, I was such a hypocrite by telling her that she was not saved, and she should read the Bible. My mother was angry, hurt, and I think a little frightened by my behavior. I knew my secrets were a form of bondage, and I began to realize the power of confession would be the beginning of my healing.

So, I sat there, pouring out my heart to her about all the abuse from her ex-husbands-- the manipulation and deceit. She could hardly process it all. My details and confession were the start of breaking the seal the enemy had placed on my life. The enemy's bondage had kept me tied up all these years. Mom just couldn't accept all the horrifying revelations, so rather quickly she gathered her things and left. Although she reacted in anger, I understood it was guilt she felt for being naive regarding my safety and trusting me to the care of my abusers. I understood Mom felt responsible, as if it were her fault, but I knew she needed time to process everything I'd relayed.

When we reconvened, she believed I was having a nervous breakdown and needed a psychiatric evaluation. She forcibly drove me to the nearest mental health clinic to have me evaluated, even though I knew I was thinking clearly. While we were driving, I heard the Lord speak to me once again, "I've got you Paige!"

After an hour or so of answering questions from the psychiatrist and with him finding no irregularities or discrepancies in my mental or emotional faculties, I was discharged. I began sharing my faith with the counselor who was evaluating me. He found my story of my visit with God fascinating. I told him the Lord had shown me my life with all the bad decisions and choices I had made, and that God had shown up to save me.

The psychiatrist walked out of our meeting to explain to my mother that I was okay mentally and had checked out as normal. My mother was dumbfounded at the diagnosis. Now, she was forced to either accept my intervention story or remain in her lack of faith. There was something alive about my story, and she knew it.

That night I experienced visions of Mom and Dad's lives, which God followed with the emotion of disappointment and sadness. He was not at all pleased with their past, and I felt His emotion of discontentment. Shortly after this, I saw a cartoonish vision of a broom behind my parents. My Lord was sweeping up the long trail of sin in their lives. Again, my right eye blinked once for yes followed by a chime. Inside my heart, I knew exactly what the meaning was. The Lord told me, "I am doing it for you."

Struck by the awe and wonder of His grace and mercy I then asked, "Lord, for what reason did you visit me and what is the ultimate purpose?" Suddenly, I saw what seemed like millions of stars that I knew represented people out in the universe, in all different directions.

Once I realized what I was seeing, God began to zoom in on one tiny star way off in the distance that was nearly covered by all the other stars. This is what He said: "Because you are the only one." To this day I am not completely sure what He meant by that statement. I suppose when it is time for me to know He will show me. With God giving each believer the gift of the Holy Spirit, He can ensure each of His children feels as like the *only one,* but I knew He meant something much greater than this. I was left with the impression that whatever it would be is something extremely powerful and unique. Regardless, I felt a love that I'd never realized before. It didn't replace the punishment of seeing Hell, which was still fresh in my mind. But I was able to know my Lord's grace, mercy and intention in a deeper way.

Chapter 22

Confession with Peace

"'In the last days, God says, I will pour out my Spirit on all
people. Your sons and daughters will prophesy, your young
men will see visions, your old men will dream dreams. Even
on my servants, both men and women, I will pour out my
Spirit in those days, and they will prophesy."
Acts 2:17-18 NIV

A day or so after my mother left, John was still concerned
about my behavior, so he telephoned his parents. While he
was talking with his parents, God began to reveal things to
me about his family. These were revelations I didn't know
and would never have known if the Lord had not revealed
them to me. During this time, God kept stressing the Father
/ Son relationship and reverence for the Father and the Son.
At the time, I wasn't quite sure what He meant. Now, I know
God is not pushy and does not force us to believe in Jesus
as Lord. At that time, I struggled with doubt of the validity of
the Holy Scriptures and questioning if Jesus was the only
way to heaven. The Father and Son emphasis during that
call to his parents was surely impressing upon my heart that
Jesus is Lord; and all that was written about Him in scripture
is the truth. There is no other Gospel apart from the one I
had heard.

I was reminded of my trip to California and the *Playboy*
mansion, when I had cheated on John. God had instructed
me to confess this to him, along with telling him about the
sexual abuse. Then God shared a vision of my boyfriend

shortly after we began dating. In the vision, he was cheating on me while he was in Las Vegas. As soon as I could digest what I was seeing, I immediately cried, "No, please! No, not again! He will hate me if I confess, I know." While my boyfriend remained in the kitchen, the Lord comforted me by telling me that we would get married. Then I saw both of us standing before the church's altar, and repeating the words, "I do."

A very clear voice of the Lord stated, "You will have two sons." He did not specify John would be the Father, but, of course, that was my assumption. Two things, I have learned about our Lord is when He tells you to do something, you had better listen, or life will become increasingly unbearable until you do. and His word will never return void. Although there are delays in our eyes, His timing is perfect. To this day, I am still awaiting the fulfillment of this message from the Lord.

Following the obedience, Angels will always be there to minister to you because of your faithfulness to the Lord. That's when you'll realize your greater good and love is always at the heart of God's direction. God comforted me about the talk He directed me to have with my boyfriend. He reassured me He would be with me. Again, the Lord said to me, "It all comes down to faith, Paige." Throughout the entire visit, faith was stressed more than anything else.

The Lord had continuously placed me in situations to test my faith. Afterward, He proved He would come through each time. His rescue may have been what I thought to be the last minute, but it always happened without fail because it was in His time. God never let me down.

Just like the conversation with Mom, my words had begun flowing without my control. I realized I couldn't change the vocabulary or sentence structure flowing from my mouth. It didn't matter what strength or thought, or effort I tried to muster. My thoughts were not synchronized with my brain. The Lord took over in each situation.

After I confessed to John, at first, he was angry. But his voice was silenced. I witnessed him supernaturally changing from anger to calmness before he rolled over on his side and went to sleep. It was shocking to see this occur. But within a few minutes as in other like situations, God showered me with a divine sense of peace, which only confirmed His presence and ability to accomplish anything on a supernatural level. God was never forceful; yet, He had a certain sternness that made me know He meant business.

It was never clear why the Lord wouldn't speak to John to validate my declarations. As I was attempting to convince him, my senses were heightened. I realized he could not comprehend my actions because he was not spiritually discerning. He also recognized I was a different person. In the days that followed, our conversations and disagreements were being controlled by God. Our words and thoughts didn't match. Odd as it may sound, it was happening for the both of us. Inside my heart, I knew God oversaw the conversation and was teaching us how to disagree Biblically on a plane much higher than the human brain can comprehend. In a split second, I knew exactly how to settle disagreements the way God wanted.

We proceeded with consideration of each other's feelings, love, and kindness. Amazing things can happen when you consider the other person's feelings. Vivid visions of a marriage with obedient and Godly Christians protecting their mate's heart was totally a new concept to me. Just give in and go to bed happy, just like the Bible tells us to do! It is amazing!

"God, why aren't you visiting John, too?" I asked.

My boyfriend quipped, "Snap out of it, Paige."

I pleaded, "God, please help me!"

Just then I saw a vision of his mother and father in a hotel room handing him my diamond ring. "Tell him you know about the diamond ring in his backpack. Tell him his mom and dad gave it to him in the hotel room during their visit last month." I could see the hotel, the day, the time, and details surrounding these statements I was uttering. "Tell him his mother gave him his grandmother's diamond ring because he did not have the money to buy a ring."

John accused me of nosing through his belongings until he realized I would not have known the details without his parents sharing this information. His parents would never divulge this information to me, so at that point, he knew I was telling the truth, but he wouldn't admit it. So, God began revealing additional facts about his family for me to relay. Keep in mind I had no idea about any of this until that moment. I was so excited and surprised that I could not contain myself. The Lord allowed my excitement for a few minutes before calming me to move forward to the next lesson. I will never forget those moments as long as I live because they were so strongly engraved in my mind.

Chapter 23

After the Rewiring

"Then Jesus came to them and said, 'All authority in heaven
and on earth has been given to me. Therefore, go and
make disciples of all nations, baptizing them in the name of
the Father and of the Son and of the Holy Spirit,
and teaching them to obey everything I have commanded
you. And surely, I am with you always,
to the very end of the age.'"
Matthew 28: 18-20 NIV

After what I refer to as *my rewiring*, God began showing visions of future things to come. I was at a car dealership purchasing a Jaguar. Next, I was sitting in a red Corvette beside my husband, but I didn't see his face. The funny thing is I didn't care about either car as my focus was on God. I saw a black car that appeared to be a BMW, rounding the corner of my neighborhood, and a black mailbox from a very affluent lakefront neighborhood in our area.

The Lord showed me that sanctification must be reached prior to the visions coming to pass. I felt a tug on my hand again and was led to the computer where, "You are a winner" flashed across the screen. I had won something but wasn't sure what it was. Could it be a prize? I'm not sure when or where this takes place, but I believe it unfolds at some point in the future. It was clear that my life radically changed after this "winning" took place.

On June 11, 2011, I was awakened by the Holy Spirit saying, "God has chosen you." I turned to stare out the window and began seeing visions of myself on stage in front of thousands of people. I was speaking about Jesus. I never saw my husband's face, but I felt his support. In the vision, we had a wonderful marriage and were enjoying the finer things in life. But we were not at all consumed by these things. My spirit was on fire for Jesus; nothing else mattered to me if I were not serving Him. Both my husband and I were passionate about sharing the Gospel and completely out of the world's ideology. What does this mean?

Please understand the material things mean nothing to me; God knows this because He knows my heart. Honestly, He was showing me that people's prayers are not bold enough. They keep themselves in legalistic bondage. I saw visions of people all over the world who were allowing Satan to talk them out of their dreams. God told me I could come boldly into His presence. Also, keep in mind because of my lack of Biblical knowledge, I didn't know anything about Paul writing these same statements in scripture.

Back to the visitation in 2002, the next vision I received was taking place on the set of a morning talk show like *Good Morning America*. A news anchor was questioning me, but I never heard the conversation. I looked and felt great, as if I were on top of the world but not consumed by it. All the wrongs I had harbored inside for so long were made right. Restoration had come. Finally, I was able to celebrate my life in a state of peace I'd never experienced before. Although I could elaborate much further on this, and will at some point, I wanted to ensure this vision was added to this account. However, God never presented a timeline.

Today, I believe more than ever that each of these visions will come to pass. Writing my testimony in this book is a way of documenting it prior to beginning this period in my life. While the visions showed I was accumulating lots of wealth, I wasn't absorbed in material things; rather, I was dedicated to giving my life and wealth to others. And we know that kingdom work requires kingdom finances.

As the visitation continued, there were fleeting moments when it seemed God had disappeared and wasn't speaking to me. Funny, He was teaching me to keep my mouth shut. He allowed me to speak without prayerfully considering my words only to myself. This lesson illustrated what happens when acting out of self-will and not His divine will. He taught me *simplicity* is best. For example, God corrected me whenever I used a harsh tone with John, or He would block harmful or unnecessary statements before I blurted them.

God's presence was evident as He controlled several arguments between us to demonstrate how easily differences could be lessened by gentleness, compassion, and not trying be right. He said we both were used to justifying our actions to no avail. Because we were not coming from a Biblical perspective, neither of us understood the other person's point of view. That's why it was easy to begin arguing about past events. We were pride-centered; we were not allowing God to be first in our lives. He taught me how easy it was to just concede and allow grace to win. It wasn't important for me to be right. God instructed the man is the spiritual head of the house. Whenever I attempted to go back and forth with Him with questions as to why I had to be submissive, God very gently showed me that it should be mutual. Woman was designed to be the man's helper and to be supportive. He said, "Submission is the highest form of love."

While lying in bed one night and praying, the Lord said, "Do not wrap your mind with religious ideology or fancy prayers accompanied by big words but come to Him with child-like faith. I know your needs before you ask." He showed me how to bring His presence into our lives. At the time, however, I was clueless as to why He was doing this, but now I know. Now, when I worship like this, I feel His presence very strongly and long for it. Even in conversation with others, I will feel His presence come over me and know it is Him. It is a very distinct feeling. Once you feel it you will never want to live without it.

God taught me the importance of rest. One of the last days of His visit as I was resting on my bed, I noticed my breath was being controlled, which was weird, but I realized God was going to teach me another lesson. He would relax my body and with a deep breath, He'd ask me to say, "Praise You Lord," on the inhale and "Thank You Father" on the exhale. This continued for a while until I realized the simplicity of worship and prayer. He said, "Praise You Lord, thank You Father." No matter how hard I tried to add words to it, He returned me to the deep breathing where I heard, "Praise You Lord" on the inhale, and "Thank you Father" on the exhale. After this continued for about thirty minutes, He appreciated the praise and simplicity of my words. And there are other things that influence His presence and ear to our prayers and worship. I would later learn the enemy has a counterfeit for that which is powerful in our prayer lives. If Christians only knew the power of just breathing and praising our Lord, they would be superpowers in His kingdom. I will say that "Contemplative Prayer" is something utilized by the New Age adherents, but there is a tremendous difference in what I was shown versus this practice. First, they aren't worshipping the same 'god;' and second, they are not praising and thanking, but instead, they are clearing their minds and unknowingly yielding their minds to demons.

On the next to last day of God's visit, I saw a clear vision of myself in a beautiful, flowing white wedding dress. I looked like a fairy tale bride waiting for her groom. My face was radiant and gleaming. At first, I thought this vision was referencing marriage to John; however, this was far beyond words.

Imagine a figure-eight pattern. I started at the bottom of the figure-eight with a man, but I never saw his face. It was as if God were asking me if I were happy with this one. I shook my head and said, "No." I was wisped to the first intersection in the figure-eight pattern where I met another man. Again, when asked if I were happy with this one, I said, "No." At the next intersection, I saw the boyfriend I would soon marry. My love for him was great, so I assumed we would stop there. Suddenly, in a whirlwind, I met another man of great stature, much different than all the others; but I never saw his face. With the same feeling I had when I saw that brilliant white light after experiencing Hell, I began drifting in soft, delicate circles from the wispy flittering green grass on Earth, high into the sky and through space. Then I disappeared into the clouds.

Chapter 24

God is Love

"And we have come to know and believe the love that God
has for us. God is love; whoever abides in love abides in
God, and God in him. And so, we know and rely on the love
God has for us. God is love"
1 John 4:16 NIV

Once again, God began to examine my heart, but this time
it was on a more intense level. I had never read scripture
regarding the examination of our hearts revealing our true
intentions. I was returned to my childhood to a scene at
my fourth birthday party. Although no one knew, I was so
embarrassed when my father entered the room. He was
fresh out of jail because he had lost his pharmacy license
because he had sold prescription drugs over the counter in
his pharmacy.

Then I heard Mom fighting with Dad non-stop over petty
issues. Each weekend, I watched as he passed out on the
floor from drinking liquor. God revealed the pain in my heart.
Then He zoomed back and placed a symbolic healed heart
over my broken one. Suddenly, the physical reality of the
sadness and pain was replaced with a flood of love – one
that feels deeper, stronger, and more secure than any feeling
of love ever known.

On the last day of the Lord's visit, I was in the shower
when I heard Him say, "It's time to go." I felt this deep sadness
race through my veins to the center of my heart. I started
pleading with God to not leave, "No, please, please don't

leave me." After a slight pause He said, "I will always be with you." Although I knew this, I also knew it was not the same. I knew what He meant. There would be time in my future when the anointing and power I had experienced would return. For nearly a week and a half, the Creator of the universe was leading each step, speaking on my behalf, controlling the environment, and showing me visions, signs, and wonders I could never have known. That would be His last sentence spoken to me until 2010.

Since God's visit, I have had to go through much testing, developing, and persevering, but I would do it again and again to be with Him. Our God is so faithful and, quite frankly, I do not know how others live without Him. It is not bragging or trying to seem divinely superior, I'm just trying to tell you that if you have not prepared for eternity, you should not wait another minute. Salvation is not only by confessing Jesus Christ as your Savior; it is truly believing in Him with all of your heart. I can assure you your heart will be tested. You will give an account for everything you have done on earth! Think long and hard because Hell is real and waiting to add your soul as its newest member.

If you have accepted Jesus, and you are prepared to meet Him, let me confirm your faith and tell you death is only a blink of an eye to a beautiful life with the Lord. When you cross over from life to death, your Heavenly Father will be waiting with open arms and with the gift of eternal life. Just look at the beautiful blue sky and know that the path you have chosen is not all you think it may be. Heaven is a million times more. Over the years, I have read the Bible cover to cover and found numerous scriptures to reference what God did during His visit with me. Each time I open the Bible, the beauty of God's word overwhelms me.

Chapter 25

Share the Good News

"However, as it is written: 'What no eye has seen, what no
ear has heard, and what no human mind has conceived" -
the things God has prepared for those who love him -
1 Corinthians 2:9 NIV

The Bible describes Heaven as a place of untold joy, worship, love, and fellowship. It is a place where there will be no more pain, tears, or sin. I look forward to this place as I have experienced all these struggles to the point of death. The Book of Revelation describes a great city of gold, magnificent in size, and the Lord Himself will be the light that shines upon it. Heaven is also a place that few find, for the path is narrow and the journey is difficult (Matthew 7:13-14).

I had experienced Hell on Earth and fully understood the wrath I would have endured had God not shown me the truth and rescued me from my sins. People have no idea what lies on the other side. They are blinded by their sin, the pursuit of pleasure, and the business and busyness of life.

If every believer could experience even two minutes of Hell, we would be pleading with our friends, loved ones, and other people to reconsider their lives and make the necessary changes. There is an incredible story, a parable of sorts, that tells the story of the callousness in our attitudes towards the lost.

As a believer, picture yourself driving down a dark, winding road late at night. It appears your car is the only one on the road. It is pouring rain, and the visibility is poor.

Every turn is almost a 90 degree turn. Danger mounts as the fog creeps in. Your heart is racing as you understand the danger involved and the need for you to slow down. All of a sudden, your car abruptly stops around a blind corner. You are out of gas; there are no visible gas stations around, and you recall there are no stations for miles. Plus, your cell phone dies! You climb out of your car and walk to the front of it. In your disbelief, there is a 500 feet drop-off to the ravine below, only two feet in front of your car. You notice the bridge is completely gone. You never saw this dangerous situation because of the rain and poor visibility. If you had not run out of gas at that precise moment, you would have fallen to your death. Your life would have been over! Suddenly, you realize there are other cars that may be coming behind you. The drivers will be unable to see your car until it's too late. Their cars will plummet into the darkness below. With flashlight in hand, you decide to walk down the road to warn oncoming vehicles of the danger. As you arrive at a good location for vehicles to see, you're reminded of two choices: 1) You can wave your flashlight and jump out in front of the traffic to warn others of the unforeseen danger or 2) You can wave at the cars passing by. After all, you wouldn't want to offend anyone or inconvenience anyone by stopping the driver, right? After all, each driver may not even believe you or may even think you're crazy! These are your two choices as you know for a fact the bridge is out. Unless you warn people, they will not be able to stop until it is too late.

While this may seem like an extreme example, it paints a valid point and explains the churches' apathy to the lost and the churches' reluctance to share the Good News for fear of being called crazy, racist, intolerant, or *Jesus freaks*. If this resembles you, I pray this book about my experience will change your mind. Let us spread the Good News of Jesus Christ and Heaven! It is not meant to be the best kept secret.

Chapter 26

My Broken Heart

"So do not fear, for I am with you; do not be dismayed, for
I am your God. I will strengthen you and help you; I will
uphold you with my righteous right hand."
Isaiah 41:10 NIV

In 2004, God visited me again while I was sleeping. His purpose was to show me a clear vision of Daddy passing away. During the visit, I saw Dad's glasses with my grandfather's face appearing through the glass frame. Immediately, I realized this was symbolic of my Father in Heaven. Telepathically, I comprehended what the Lord was saying. Once it fully registered, my grandfather's face crumbled in the frame. Suddenly, I heard myself screaming. Unstoppable tears were streaming from the four corners of my eyes.

At this point in time, John and I had married. It was late and he was still watching television, until he heard my screams. He flew into the room and grabbed me to comfort me – in the flesh. But as he did, something else began to penetrate my being, relaxing me as if the dream had never happened. This could only be a divine sense of peace. Within minutes I had fallen back into a deep and peaceful sleep.

Two years later, when I was thirty-three, my dad passed away on October 14, 2006. It was also my mother's birthday. His death broke my heart. Unfortunately, I'd seen signs that Daddy had relapsed and was drinking, but not to the extent it had been before the Twelve Step program when he would stay inebriated, drunk all the time. My son, Parker, had just been born, and I was overjoyed and totally absorbed with being a new mother. Whenever we were together every other week when I took him to get groceries and to doctors' appointments, he was fine and didn't drink. But since I had been a little girl, I'd remained observant, protective, and in tune with his health. I had noticed he seemed to be declining rapidly. Daddy had that *alcohol face.* You understand what I'm talking about: the big red nose and the pits in his face. To me it seemed like a rapid decline, but in all fairness, it may have taken a while for his appearance and body to change, but Dad never talked about his health or anything like that.

When Dad got sober, he stayed that way for eight years. These were the best eight years of my life. You see, I'm a lot like my father. He had so many spiritual gifts he could have given this world, but the enemy used the college fraternities and partying friends to keep him in bondage. After graduation, he was unable to break free from the enemy's grasp, becoming a highly functioning alcoholic throughout his life until his sobriety for eight years. When I was introduced to the real man beneath the alcohol, I was delighted and amazed to finally know my father. He was brilliant and interesting, and I loved him very much.

I had noticed the telltale signs of regression, my heart broke. When I hadn't heard from Daddy in six days, there was a deep gnawing in my soul. It was that *knowing* that something was wrong. One of my worst fears was that I'd be the one to discover him whenever he passed. But thanks to God, that did not occur and I was spared from the pain.

Don't get me wrong. I'm good under pressure and intense situations, but thankfully, God spared me this time. After laying Parker in his crib to nap, I telephoned my husband. When he answered, I cried, "Please go check on Dad. I'm unable to get him on the phone. It's been a couple of hours.

I can't get him to answer the phone."

It had been six days since I had heard from him. The last time was when I'd taken him to have his cataracts removed. I'll never forget how excited he was to see so well once again. "I have a new set of eyes!" he kept repeating.

Thankfully John was able to enter dad's house through an unlocked window. He found his lifeless body on the couch and called 911. After forty minutes of resuscitation, the medics were only able to achieve a heart beat. Then they rushed him to the hospital for further evaluation and stability.

This entire time, I had been home alone and hadn't received any contact. I'd telephoned several times, but my husband wouldn't answer the phone. That's when I just knew and began pouring tears. I tried to call Mom, who was on a cruise to Alaska. I tried calling my aunt. I tried calling my best friend. No one answered. It was just God and me. I laid in the floor and cried and cried. Then I cried out to God. I needed to leave. I needed to go to my father.

When I finally received the call from my husband, he was riding in the back of the ambulance with my dad to the hospital. He stated they were able to get a heartbeat, which seemed so encouraging and gave me hope. I needed to go. I was going to take Parker with me to the hospital until I happened to receive a call from our nanny. I cried, "Juju, would you please come here?" Quickly, I told her about Dad. "I've got to go." She was there in no time. I look back and see how that time with the Lord was so precious and intentional. I was able to cry out to Him. Boy was it painful trying to get someone on the phone.

After I arrived at the hospital, the doctor came to me and said, "Ms. Coffey, your father suffered a massive heart attack. We were able to get your dad's heart beating, but I have some bad news. It doesn't look like there is any brain activity whatsoever. We're going to run tests."

When the doctors returned, the brain scan had shown there was no activity. "If we keep him on these machines and monitors, that's all it will be. They will just keep his heart beating. That's all."

I cried, "I just can't let him go. Can I spend the night with him?"

"Yes, but in the morning, we will need to run tests to see if there is any response at all. These tests will be invasive, but you will have the opportunity to witness them and know for yourself."

This was such a special gift from the Lord. I was able to lie beside my father and talk to him, hold his hand, and tell him how much I loved him, all the while hoping to see a sign – any sign whatsoever that he was alive. I could hear his heart beating, but there was nothing else. Fairly early the next morning when the doctors arrived, I remained in the room while they did the tests, which were horrible, just horrible, but this proved to me Daddy was gone. My mother's birthday was October 14, so I truly believe that is the day when he left. When the medics were able to get a heartbeat, I believe that was all they got. I joked with my father's corpse. "If there was a day that you could have departed, it would be Mom's birthday." Surrounded by doctors, nurses, and my husband, I watched through brimming tears as they turned off the machines, one by one. Sympathetically, they turned to me. I kissed my father and said goodbye. My father's death was a horrific experience and very traumatic time in my life. Doctors and nurses and my ex-husband were there with me when they turned off the machines.

***

I've often wished I had siblings, but I especially wished I had them to help me plan for my father's funeral. These sad plans were mine to make – alone – and that made it difficult. There have been lots of circumstances and opportunities in my life when I've had to go it alone. I had to be strong. In many cases, I was forced to be strong. This was a really difficult time, working through the pain and trauma. Somehow, I made it through picking out the casket, talking with the funeral home, and going step by step. I saw the true colors of my father's family. No one from his family attended – not even his brothers. My paternal grandmother had already passed away in 2001. It was my mother's side of the family who attended the service.

***

Shortly before his death, Dad had relapsed and begun drinking again. When I entered his empty house where his absence screamed loudly within its walls, I found confirmation of his relapse with a bottle of alcohol lying on the floor beside the sofa where the Lord had received his spirit. But beside the bottle was a Bible.

For years, I did not know what the outcome was for my father's soul. So, I prayed and prayed asking the Lord to show me. Somehow, I had always believed that finding the Bible was the Lord's way of confirming the promise He had made to me. During the visitation in 2002 He assured me that Dad and Mom would be saved.

Finally, in answer to my prayers, the Lord gave me a dream through which the Almighty spoke, "The day of your father's death was the day of his redemption."

Chapter 27

The Vine

"He fulfills the desires of those who fear him; he hears their cry and saves them. The LORD watches over all who love him, but all the wicked he will destroy"
Psalm 145:19-20 NIV

Years after God's visit in 2002, while longing to know what I was to do for Him, He gave me a beautiful dream. One night prior to going to bed, I asked the Holy Spirit to give me an indication of where I was on my journey with Him. At 4:30 a.m., I was awakened by a dream with a song playing in the background. God began pulling everything together for me. In the dream I walked into a convenience store looking for seeds to plant. An old man behind the counter approached me asking if he could help determine which seeds to buy. Not knowing much about planting or harvesting, I humbly agreed and accepted his assistance. Though I didn't know much about this topic, I did know that if I planted the wrong seeds, I would get a snake instead of a luscious green plant or vine.

Around us, other people had harvested vines or snakes. It seemed like a game show where contestants wait with anticipation to find whether they got a hit or miss. For whatever reason, the vines would grow immediately if you received the correct seed. They grew to the height of a tall bush or small tree, depending on the type of seed. I planted a few seeds, but nothing happened. Suddenly, I hit the jackpot. My vine shot into the sky and up through the clouds. I was reminded of "Jack and the Beanstalk."

This was the thickest, tallest vine I had ever seen. Right away, I recognized this was God's work. The old man was the Holy Spirit and of course the vine was symbolic of Jesus Christ, "The Vine." As I laid there processing the dream, I thanked God for the answer and asked Him a question: "Why did you leave me?" His response was, "Well, it was your fault." God was being funny because he knew I'd understand exactly what it meant. I sure had missed His sense of humor.

I had closed the book on my testimony and turned the other cheek because I had so much to do. This was representative of another request I made to God. I asked Him to show His wittiness again because I missed it. I had been asking Him, "Why did you leave me?" and "What am I missing here?" Then all the signs from God He had already given began to surface – the signs to complete my testimony, but I had missed them. That's when God said, "Get it done!"

My daughter was twelve years old at that time. She had brought many beautiful pieces of artwork home for me to enjoy; however, the week of the beanstalk dream she handed me the picture of a giant beanstalk, which she'd made in art class. She had colored this picture of a giant vine stretching high up into the sky. Of course, I hadn't shared the dream with her, but instantly I knew it was another sign from the Lord. I was smiling from ear to ear.

Chapter 28

The 700 Club

"As obedient children do not conform to the evil desires you had when you lived in ignorance"
1 Peter 1:14 NIV

In 2010 after my visit from the Lord and some fine tuning of my spirit, the Lord spoke to me in a dream. He told me to submit my visit with Him and my testimony to three ministries: *The* 700 Club, the *Sid Roth Show* and *Joyce Meyer*. They all responded, but it was the 700 Club personnel who pursued me and wanted me on their program.

Over the course of the next few months, I was interviewed over the phone five different times by *The 700 Club*. Each interview was like climbing a rung in a ladder. It was the process of having my testimony aired. Each time I had an interview, I spoke with a different person. Obviously, it was a screening process to eliminate fake conversions and people, who just wanted to be seen on television. Of course, I initially thought people I talked with had the impression I was crazy, *off my rocker.* They kept the interview process alive, wanting to know all about my visit.

"How did you know it was from God and not the enemy?" I was asked several times.

"I just knew it was all from the Lord and that all He showed me radically changed my life for the better." After all, Satan came only to steal, kill, and destroy, so the visit only made sense through the beauty and restoration of the Lord.

My mother was concerned that the broadcast would

paint a bad picture of her, portraying her as a villain. Initially, Mom didn't want me to mention her at all. Thankfully, she later conceded.

"It makes you look good, but not me!" she exclaimed. Although I knew she was upset at the time, I also knew the Lord's hands were on it, and redemption would be experienced all around, including by my mother.

In the end, the airing of the episode did place a large strain on our relationship off and on for around five years. I totally understand she was operating off a tremendous amount of guilt and needed time to heal. Often, she would remind me she didn't want to discuss it; and she didn't want her name brought up in company when anyone was discussing my story.

After I confessed the abuse to Mom, she had experienced many mixed emotions. She was angry she didn't know about the sexual abuse and how it had occurred right beneath her nose. It took some time for her to begin healing. Even today, I know the Lord is still working in both of our hearts. We have fully reconciled and understand how God used our pain and suffering to pour goodness into the lives of others. My mother had given her heart to the Lord in 2004 after a cancer scare, and she loves Him dearly and continues to grow in him daily.

After nearly a full year of interviews, an executive producer, Debbie White, telephoned me, deciding to move forward with my story. At the time, I was living in Matthews, North Carolina, and attending seminary. In addition, I was working hard to support my family. *The 700 Club* flew a film crew to my home. In addition, we used several other locations, including the local Chestnut Oak Playground to film various scenes of my family and me.

The film crew was there two days, filming up to seven hours straight over the interview process. Debbie White interviewed me, asking the same questions I had answered in my twenty-five-page testimony. Her main concern was depicting the right story, which would capture the redemptive nature of my visit. Ms. White explained there was so much information, she could have made a series from it. My neighbor, Hope, whom I was counseling at the time and helping her to interpret dreams she was having, lived beside me from 2010-2013. She was also interviewed by *The 700 Club* as a character witness. They were interested in what had happened to me since my visit with the Lord – how had it changed me for the better. Hope's interview only strengthened my testimony to Debbie and solidified the airing of the episode.

The day Debbie White and the film crew left, she asked me to pray for the correct storyline that God wanted presented to the world. She also asked me to share any videos/pictures of my life, which could be used in the production. After many months of silence from the Lord, I was excited to see my story visually. I deeply wanted to share my story to so many so I could help change lives and give others hope when all hope is lost.

Right before the episode aired, Debbie called me and said, "I did the best I could. I hope you are happy with it." Then she explained they had decided to focus on the Heaven and Hell portion of my story and sharing the Gospel instead of the supernatural occurrences." She informed me they were integrating my testimony into their Heaven and Hell series because it was a perfect fit. Their plans to air the episode would be done during their "Sweeps Week, a week set aside during each year to increase ratings."

When the episode aired on October 12, 2012, the Lord stepped in again. On the previous day, Hurricane Sandy had devastated the East Coast, so many people were home and in need of hope as the storm had caused catastrophic damage. Many people were afraid and felt lost, even hopeless, so they were seeking a spiritual boost. As a result, millions of people tuned in to watch *The 700 Club* and my testimony.

After the episode aired, Debbie called me for a follow-up. She shared it was one of their most popular and most viewed episodes. This thrilled me that my pain and redemption had been viewed by so many. Hopefully, my story had given them hope to move ahead in their lives.

Several weeks after the airing, Debbie White telephoned again to share good news. "Because of the popularity of your episode, may we use it again on our "Partner's Club" Video?" She was referring to a DVD package *The 700 Club* would send to anyone willing to become a donation partner with their ministry. The video featured the top ten testimonies of the year; mine was the first one. While it was humbling, I knew God was using my testimony to help others.

I began receiving speaking engagement offers from several churches and small groups around the Charlotte area. My email inbox was inundated with emails. Relatives called. Strangers in stores would approach me, asking if I was the woman from *The 700 Club* video. This was shocking, yet delightful, knowing God's message was being heard and He was using me to fulfill His Divine purpose. Finally, I had reached a place in my life journey where I understood my purpose in life; I was being called into full-time ministry.

Chapter 29

Seminary or Bust

"When your words came, I devoured them;
they were my joy and my heart's delight,
for I bear your name, Lord God Almighty"
Jeremiah 15:16 NIV

Following the beanstalk dream, I knew it was time to heavily pursue my calling and kingdom purpose. I became ravenous for God's Word and read every opportunity, never getting enough. I meditated on it often. On weekends, when my daughter was with her father, I would spend the entire weekend with God, praying, fasting, and reading His Word. Seldom, if ever, did I turn on the television because I didn't want to waste any time that could be better spent getting to know my Creator better. It was during this time, what I refer to as *Navy Seal training* in the spirit, when I found the power of fasting.

During this period, the Lord was leading me through a heavy sanctification process. He was clearing out all the junk -- there was a lot to clean out. Years of abuse, poor decisions, and sin had hardened my heart and given the enemy open doorways into my life. These doorways needed to be closed and the enemy evicted! God was stripping me down to nothing! In January of 2010, I was sitting on the edge of my bed one night, reading my Bible and I heard the Lord say, "You are going to seminary."

Without reservation or hesitation, I answered, "Of course I will; anything you desire my Lord." I had no idea when or how it would happen, but I knew God had spoken and His word does not return void. I had never finished college, but longed for that sense of accomplishment in my life. As a child, my grandmother Coffey always hung the education my cousins received over my head. I knew in my heart that I didn't measure up in her eyes. Those she approved of were going to be doctors or lawyers; they graduated from the prestigious universities. She would make foul comments about my mother and ostracized my father for being the one that rebelled. Too many people, including my now ex-husband, said I would never amount to anything. I remember those hurtful words. "You're just a dumb blonde." "What school would ever want you?" But I knew the Lord had spoken to me, so the next day, I started my search for the school I would attend. I needed one that would work for a single mother with two children, but nothing seemed to fit that I could afford.

At the time, I was selling skin care products for a skincare and nutraceutical company. This job allowed me to work from home while caring for my family. I answered God. "Okay, Lord, I will go to seminary as soon as I have the money to go." After I spoke to God regarding seminary with my plans to wait until I had the money to attend, my business dried up. Shortly thereafter I was almost completely out of work. When God has closed a door there is no amount of holding it open or prying it back open that will work. The question remained, *How am I going to attend school and support my family without cash?*

With the next semester starting soon, I knew God was telling me to go now. It was at that point I knew selling everything I could and picking up my cross to follow Him was going to be a realized material fact in my life. This was no longer Paige's life with God helping her along the way. This new life would have to be sold out in word and deed. I needed to act. The only things I really had of value to sell were two sentimental items that had significance in my life: a wedding ring from my prior marriage and my dad's antique Grand Prix. With tears of sadness, I contacted a diamond broker to sell my ring. She was readily able to meet me and offered a fair price for the diamond. The Lord would often wake me with lyrics to songs. He knew I was somber about having to sell my ring so the following morning I was awakened by the song, "A Whole New World" by Peabo Bryson. I knew it was His way of saying, "Pick up your cross and follow me into this whole new world." To this day, He still uses songs in the night, morning, or various times throughout the day. Sometimes I must reference the lyrics as it could be a song I haven't heard in years. Often, it is a song that is special to Him and me; it is a reminder of His love and leading on this wild and crazy journey through life.

After I sold the ring, I proceeded to find the right buyer for my dad's Grand Prix. I pray the one who purchased the car loves it as much as Dad and Granddaddy once did. Once I finally had the funds to pay my bills and first semester of school, I applied to Southern Evangelical Seminary, one of the top schools in the country for apologetics. It was exciting to begin my *education*. Never could I imagine the amount of religion that was being taught on this level, but it was also necessary for me to learn where the church was presently and where it was going in the future. Exactly one year later in January 2011, my acceptance letter from Southern Evangelical Seminary arrived. I began my first semester shortly thereafter. Little did I know I had only started my journey of sacrifice. My years of selling anything in my home of value followed those years of education.

Throughout each semester of the six long years of seminary, the Holy Spirit spoke to me through various visions and dreams more than ever before. In 2016 I graduated from seminary as Suma Cum Laude and Valedictorian of my class with a 3.98 GPA. That's not bad for the dumb blonde I was always portrayed to be. It was an incredible accomplishment for me and brought a sense of accomplishment, as well as justice to those who challenged what I could do in Christ.

The Lord had put me through six rewarding years of schooling which was one of the most challenging times of my life. Often overwhelmed and exhausted from exertion and lack of sleep, I worked nights, weekends and holidays to help pay bills and support my two children.

Chapter 30

Groundbreaking

"Come to me, all you who are weary and burdened,
and I will give you rest.
Take my yoke upon you and learn from me,
for I am gentle and humble in heart,
and you will find rest for your souls.
For my yoke is easy and my burden is light."
Matthew 11:28-30 NIV

In July 2012, while attending seminary, I started a radio broadcast. The Lord had given me a dream about being on the radio and helping those in need. I wanted confirmation about what I was about to do, so I asked Him for more dreams. He gave them to me. There was only one radio station near me, which was WSIC in North Carolina, a conservative station that featured many prominent radio hosts like Rush Limbaugh. I booked the 11 a.m. on Thursday mornings for a sixty-minute program called *Groundbreaking*. Along with a sound Biblical teaching, people would often call for dream interpretations and Biblical counseling. The airtime cost $1100 each month, but the donations from radio listeners and one of my partners in ministry, Hope, covered the costs.

This was a busy time for me -- juggling home, working nights, attending seminary, and now producing a radio show. It's amazing how I was able to do so much with so little, but the Lord always pulled me through each month to keep me going. It wasn't long before I had another dream with yet another assignment. To add to my already heavy schedule,

I had to apply to broadcasting school. This was the ultimate busy season of life.

After about a year and a half of radio, the funding dried up. God was shutting it down and moving me onto something else. The station manager abruptly shut the show down, explaining they wouldn't be able to fund me. I wasn't even allowed to say good-bye to my audience, which devastated me at the time. I had built many followers and made friends while on that show. It hurt that I wasn't allowed any time to conclude "Groundbreaking" the way I wanted to.

On the day the radio show ended, that very night I received a phone call from a prophet friend, who spoke truth to me at a time when I felt down and needed a Word from the Lord. My friend said I was a modern-day Elijah; God was leading me somewhere else, but I would be fed at the brook by God for a time before moving forward. Oddly enough, he was not even aware about the radio show shutting down when he telephoned me that night. He said the Lord would feed me by the ravens at the ravine of Kerith (1 Kings 17:1-6, NIV). I knew from this message the Lord was moving me forward and for me not to look back, but it would be a season of supernatural leading and provision. I felt refreshed, anew, and eager to learn where He would lead me next.

The next day Arroe Collins, one of my professors at broadcasting school and most accomplished radio broadcaster in our state, contacted me. He had unknowingly been listening to my radio show and loved it. The message read like this: "Your heart needs to be heard around the world. Send me your shows and I will see to it that they are." He wanted my voice to be heard around the world. Surprise! Arroe had moved away from traditional broadcasting via expensive radio shows and moved into the worldwide stations like IHeart Radio. This was a fantastic opportunity to reach more people free! God used what seemed like a huge setback and turned it into a setup for bigger and better opportunities. Never would I have imagined that someone of Arroe's caliber would have been interested in my little Groundbreaking show. I knew this could only have been orchestrated by the hand of God.

God took my $1100 per month local radio show and turned it into a worldwide blessing, for free, to be heard over twenty-six stations around the globe. Immediately, I created a small radio studio inside my home and began pouring my heart into new material for Arroe. What a blessing! It wasn't long before he sent the new demographics illustrating the reach of the show and to what areas around the globe. I recall the many emails that would pour in from people who had been touched and the great welling up of love in my heart knowing God was at work through me.

However, by 2015, I was over committed through the radio show, working nights, taking care of my family, running a women's ministry, all the while attending seminary and broadcasting school. I was burnt out; my health and overall demeanor with friends and family were affected. I knew I needed a rest. I needed a sabbatical. I needed to rejuvenate and refocus on where the Lord was taking me. The pressure of serving and pouring into the lives of others without resting in the Spirit was foreign to me. I didn't understand how not to get burnt out. How could I stop now and let anyone down that needed a touch from the Lord? But it all came to a head by the end of that year.

Once the radio broadcast was over, I stepped away from ministry completely for that season of my life. But God continued to work on me.

Around the end of 2015, God gave me another dream. In the dream, I was sitting on my couch and teaching from the Bible on my own television show! I bought a camera in 2016 and waited! Unfortunately, God gave me another dream right after the purchase, telling me to pack up all my radio equipment and the new camera then wait for the next step. Ugh! If you ever pray for something, pray for patience, too. I knew I didn't have the funding for a tv spot, so I waited on the Lord to open a door for me.

One of my greatest passions in life outside of my relationship with God is dancing. I competed throughout my school years, practicing for up to three hours a day to escape the pain I had been hiding inside my heart. The only escape I had was through dancing. Once I had my children, though, it had to go on the backburner. In 2011 I began to dance again, a class here and there, then before long I started teaching my own dance fitness class at the YMCA.

I continued the dance fitness through 2018, with a creation of my own called, "Glo Dance Fit", a choreographed dance class that became quite popular in my area. I enjoyed the relationships I made, the hard work I put in, and the overall fulfillment of dancing again. I yearned to own a place of my own and what the Lord showed me so many years ago in my visit with him. He showed me that fitness, especially dance would be a huge part of my ministry in the future.

My good friend Stephanie's grandmother, Evelyn, who is ninety years young, had a spot for ministry on the Charlotte Cable Television Network. Evelyn had been teaching the Bible on that show for almost twenty years! Stephanie reached out to me, understanding my radio and broadcasting school background, and asked me to help her grandmother with the cable show. Evelyn was aging and was having difficulty with the content and format of the program. I appeared on several episodes of that Bible teaching platform when Evelyn became ill and was unable to continue with the show. The 7 p.m. slot was a perfect time, so I became Evelyn's stand-in.

It was necessary for Stephanie to be present every Thursday as she was representing her grandmother's spot.

Evelyn's desire was that Stephanie would eventually take over the ministry and time slot on the show, but Steph didn't feel ready or led to do so at the time. She was not comfortable standing in front of a camera. Unfortunately, I was not able to take the time slot. Also, to gain a time slot, it was required that the producer must be a county resident.

As a God wink, Stephanie offered to become a producer at the television station, and we decided on an 11 a.m. time slot for Thursday, which worked out better for both of us. It was a thirty-minute show entitled, *The Coffey Shop*. This program lasted one and a half years. It was a fulfillment of everything God had shown me. I was thrilled to have the opportunity to share my story and help others grow in Christ.

I kept getting dreams from the Lord, showing me that I would someday host a syndicated television show as a *Kelly Ripa*-like hostess, but Christian instead. In this dream, my *show* would always entail a series of guests who would appear on my show to discuss their life problems with me. As I would speak to them, the Spirit of God would come out of me and heal them.

In another talk show dream, I was a Christian type of *Ellen,* helping people through their struggles and delivering them from the bondage they were in. I was a guest on a talk show in one dream, discussing the "Christian Horror Movies" I was making and exorcising demons in these films the way Jesus did during his three year-ministry. The man, who would later become my husband, stood behind me as my bodyguard, watching over me and protecting me from any harm.

After I finally graduated from seminary, I started having dreams about law school. The Lord wanted me to study for the LSAT exam, so I began a year-long intensive study in 2016 to prepare myself for law school.

I scored high enough on the LSAT exam to qualify for

acceptance into the only local law school around. During the application process, the school lost its accreditation, so my journey into law school ended. What I did not know at the time was the Lord had me doing this for a completely different reason. As usual, He had another spiritual teaching for me: the Courtrooms of Heaven! My LSAT preparation was God teaching me about the legality and courtrooms of Heaven, preparing me to help others in counseling (lots of family/legal issues), and setting the foundation for my future husband and our ministry together. God wastes nothing, so my year-long study ensued.

Chapter 31

Divine Appointment

"If you are willing and obedient,
you will eat the good things of the land."
Isaiah 1:19 NIV

While I was attending seminary, one of my jobs was as a waitress at PF Chang's. This job helped me financially to support my children and allowed me to work at night and attend school during the day. This was a fantastic experience as the owners were accommodating and super nice to me. PF Chang's was a busy restaurant, sporting over fifty-six tables, which were almost always filled.

One day shift, while I was working, it was an unusually slow day, and I only had one table. An elderly man with silver hair walked into the restaurant by himself, and the hostess *just happened* to seat him in my section. I noticed he had a familiar face. This man was Sid Roth from Sid Roth Christian Ministries on the CBN network! He had recently moved his studio to Charlotte, NC. Now, he was sitting at one of my tables! What an honor! After serving the soup he ordered, he asked me, "Do you know who I am?"

I replied, "Of course I do! You're Sid Roth!" I spent over an hour with him that day, telling him of my ministry and *The 700 Club* experience. I explained how I had originally mailed my testimony to three places: *The 700 Club, The Sid Roth Show*, and to Joyce Meyers. Sid asked me to send my testimony again, giving me special instructions on how to send it. It was a pleasure speaking with him, especially knowing God had set up this meeting and another meeting for a later time.

Again, I sent my testimony to Sid, and within days, I received a follow up phone call from his assistant. We booked a lunch together at, yes, you guessed it, PF Chang's. I spoke with his assistant, and she confirmed that Sid wanted me to be a guest on the show. Then she explained I needed to have something tangible to share with their audience, such as a book detailing my visit with God and my story. "As soon as you finish your book, get in touch with us and we'll have you on as our special guest." I complied, knowing the Lord wanted my story written to share with the world. He would place the right people in my life to accomplish this goal.

Chapter 32

God's Providence

"We know that all things work together for the good of those who love God, who are called according to His purpose."
Romans 8:28 NIV

In the summer of 2018, I received an email that was sent to the Paige Coffey Ministries Website by a man in the Boston area after he had seen *The 700 Club* video on his *Facebook* page. This seemed odd because the video had aired in October 2012 and *The 700 Club* only aired new testimonies. I am convinced he saw the video because of the Lord, whose providence was for us to meet. He also sent me a sweet message on *Facebook* messenger. This man, Doug, explained how he was inspired by my testimony and politely invited me to have coffee with him sometime. My response was, "I'm not interested in dating, but we can become friends." Doug seemed pleasantly surprised that I had responded, so we developed an online friendship over the next few months.

I learned Doug was a fifty-year-old personal trainer from New Hampshire and a former police officer. Doug was a dedicated Christ follower with obvious passion for the Lord and a strong desire to spread the Good News. Over *Facebook* messenger, we often discussed spiritual matters.

Doug planned a visit to South Carolina in August of 2018 to visit close friends from his college days. Because he'd be a few hours from my home, he invited me to meet him face-to-face over coffee, so I accepted. We agreed on a time before his flight home. Unfortunately, he encountered several highway accidents. Fearful he'd miss his flight to Boston, he drove straight to the airport. We both joke about it to this day because we were unsure if this block was from the Lord or the enemy.

Doug called and apologized, but we both agreed the missed meeting happened for a reason. With an hour to chat prior to boarding, we chatted over the phone. His disappointment was obvious but understood God had a plan, so he was more than gracious to abide by it. He explained in detail how his wife of three years had left him after an argument the previous January. Without warning, she packed her bags and left. Now, he was living through a contentious divorce, as she refused to communicate or work on saving the marriage. Doug was devastated that all efforts to reconcile were met with silence. He had invested and given up everything to be with his wife and fourteen-year-old stepdaughter.

Because I was a Biblical counselor, I explained how his story was like another my ministry partner, Hope. God uses many avenues to speak to us, and many we take for granted daily. Today His message was given in the smallest of signs: hope. Usually, I don't counsel men. I'm careful not to open a door that the possibility of any romantic interest or emotional bond would result from either side. But Doug's story was familiar, and because of his calm demeanor and spiritual maturity, I accepted him as a counselee. Deep in my heart, I believed Doug would reunite with his wife and God would use me as the facilitator.

We began our twice-a-week counseling sessions in September of 2018. Over the phone, we hammered away at his past. Doug had gone through six months of counseling with a biblical counselor in New Hampshire where his past marriage and religious spirit were discussed. He was helped through lots of loss and grieving and steered away from worldly pursuits he used to mask his pain. Gradually, Doug began to recognize his own shortcomings, but he was puzzled about his failing marriage. There had been a few issues, but his wife and he got along fairly well. They'd worked hard at building a life together.

At the end of six months, Doug amicably parted ways with his counselor and began spiritually pursuing different roads he'd never considered before. Determined to understand the demise of their marriage and what he'd done to push away his wife, he struggled to discover what was at the core of her abandonment. While he searched and researched psychological issues online, his wife wasn't interested in reconciliation and was diligently pursuing a divorce. By the summer of 2018, Doug was despondent with no hope of reuniting with his wife. His main pursuit was to understand the breakup and spiritual reasons why the Lord had seemingly abandoned him.

Doug's tireless research resulted in uncovering a series of patterns that fit their situation: narcissism. He learned the definition and discovered the traits and habits of narcissists, along with spiritual implications of relationships associated with them. Dumbfounded, he recognized eerie similarities of his wife and how she'd abandoned the marriage. Now, he was convinced he was dealing with a narcissistic spirit in his wife and wanted to know everything about it.

There are two varying definitions of true narcissism. One was a clinical diagnosis through a psychological approach. The second was totally opposite: a Christian perspective on the behavior. Defined Biblically, true narcissism is *insolent pride* or *pride on steroids*. The first sin in recorded history was the *sin of pride* when the enemy tried to convince Adam and Eve they would become like *God.* The worldly definition and treatment of narcissism does not address the spiritual roots or how to be delivered from it, and Doug knew what needed to be done.

A believer for over forty years, Doug understood the sin nature. He was biblically well-read. He attended a Christian college, had a brief stint at seminary, and shared his faith in sport by playing for the Athletes in Action basketball team in the summer of 1989. Even while Doug struggled to grow in his faith, and his sanctification process was ongoing, he loved the Lord and desired ways to tell others about the Good News of the Gospel. Equipped with Biblical knowledge, he knew the path he'd take for a full grasp of narcissism and the root issues of the sin behavior.

Doug's Internet search finally stumbled on a Christian Website that was dedicated to narcissistic behavior and everything about it. This frustrated him because for every forty Websites on narcissism, only one was Christian based. He found the information lacking as the *secular* advice was to cut and run from all narcissists and never associate with them. They were deemed an incurable people with zero chance at reconciliation.

Once he'd found the definition and spiritual explanation for narcissism, Doug needed to understand what caused it. His investigation led to a small ministry, Amadeus Ministries, which was led by Deliverance Minister, Rachelle Lamond. She had several *YouTube* videos on narcissism and the demonic cause of the behavior. As Doug hungrily devoured each video, there was a same occurring theme: the Jezebel Spirit!

The Jezebel Spirit is one of the foundational spirits for narcissism and gains entrance through open doors in our lives. Open doors, such as sexual abuse, mental/emotional abuse, trauma, habitual sin, the occult, and sexual immorality give opportunity to the enemy to enter our lives and develop this narcissistic bondage. The spiritual term for this manifestation is a *Jez-narc.* They all have similar sin patterns and live their lives through fear, throwing away all relationships, which do not fit into their own twisted way of looking at life.

Doug watched one video that described the twenty-four common traits of the *Jez-narc* manifestation. It is difficult to have healthy relationships with *Jez-narcs* because they have deceived their small trust circle surrounding them. They will lie repeatedly to protect this spirit and can believe their own lies in the process. Their game plan is a series of love-bombing, control, manipulation, the silent treatment, gaslighting, hoovering, smear campaigns, and throw away relationships. They need to be constantly adored and have few if any close relationships. People that get into Jez-narc relationships, like Doug did, have no clue to the behavior until the Lord sheds light on the person. It is an eye-opening experience once one is enlightened to the pattern of this spirit and the lengths it will go to protect itself and move on from one generation to the next. Its sole goal is to destroy those chosen for ministry and to ruin families.

Christian Jez-narcs are the most dangerous as they hide behind a false façade of moral superiority and religion. They are experts at twisting scripture and rarely, if ever, read the Bible. It's the perfect disguise to hide who they really are and can fool just about anyone who is not educated about this dangerous spirit. Doug contacted Rachelle Lamond and set up a counseling appointment with her. She was well-read Biblically and told Doug she couldn't help him any further than where he was. Although Rachelle was educated on the subject, she felt she didn't know anything more than Doug did to help him. So, she suggested he search for a counselor who primarily focused on the Jezebel spirit.

After a few more months of searching, Doug found me, thus, the beginning of our sessions together. Over the years I have become an expert on narcissistic behavior and the

Jezebel spirit. I had counseled and experienced this spirit unlike most have. I understood how to beat it. Delighted, Doug knew God put us together and was at the center of his situation. God had everything in control.

129

Chapter 33

Jezebel Calling

"Nevertheless, I have this against you:
You tolerate that woman Jezebel,
who calls herself a prophet.
By her teaching she misleads my servants
into sexual immorality
and the eating of food sacrificed to idols"
Revelation 2:20 NIV

Let me explain how I became an expert on the Jezebel spirit. This spirit had haunted me for over 40 years, so I was quite familiar with it. My first introduction with the spirit was in the ninth grade when three of my friends and I were *playing* with a Ouija board game. Interestingly, the game is made by children's game *experts*, Parker Brothers. We had zero knowledge of the occultic roots of this game or the doors that are opened to the enemy when you invite them in. My life changed after this event; it would never be the same again. The roots had gained a foothold through all the sexual abuse that occurred. But it was at this point in my life when the doors of the occult were opened.

The Jezebel spirit is first referenced in 1 Kings 16 when the evil King Ahab and his sinister wife, Jezebel, ruled over Israel at that time and brought unprecedented sin and idolatry into the land. King Ahab's wife was a conniving, manipulating, and sexually immoral woman, who used her beauty and power to rule and destroy others. Revelation 2:20 refers to this Jezebel spirit at the end of the age and how this demon will influence and destroy certain churches. It is exposed in many Christian counseling evaluations, all retaining the exact same characteristics from person to person.

This spirit is one of the chief demons. Its main duty is to destroy churches, marriages, and keep ordained Christians from ministry. It is powerful, sneaky, and can stay hidden or unnoticed for years. It is especially dangerous amongst Christians, as it hides within a deep facade of religion and fake outward obedience.

The Jezebel spirit was one of the main reasons why it took me so long to come around after God's visit in 2002. I struggled with several types of sins that it seemed like I just could not beat, no matter how hard I tried, prayed, or read the Bible. My sanctification process through the Holy Spirit was slowed by this spirit's relentless attack on my life through the doors I had opened to the demonic realm. The partying, drug use, sexual promiscuity, and overall rebellion I had through my second marriage after my visit with God was, in part, due to the control of this spirit and the negativity it had on my life. I was bound, but I didn't realize it. I dealt with systolic ovaries (PCOS) from puberty throughout my thirties, always having extreme pain and never understanding the root cause of it. Later, after learning about this demon and how it operates, I came to realize this spirit lies within the female reproductive system.

I started learning more and more about the Jezebel spirit, where it came from and that I had many of its traits. I never knew a believer could be *demonized* if they had the Holy Spirit's indwelling. My challenge was to read scripture more carefully and to find where the word *possession* originated from the Greek-to-English translations. The Greek word, *daimonizomai*, phonetic spelling, *dahee-mon-id*-zom-ahee, literally means *demonized, not possessed*. Although the Greek word doesn't entail ownership and a true believer in Christ cannot be owned by a demon, it does, in fact, mean that a believer can be tormented by a demon or demons by opening doors to the enemy through habitual sin, abuse, or generational curses.

In Matthew 12:43-45, Jesus tells of the man who is delivered from an evil spirit, how the man is swept clean, and how his house was put in order. It is obvious the man who Jesus is referring to had a salvation experience from the *cleaned-up house*. The demon goes out, gets seven more demons, more powerful than itself, and returns to the man who ends up much worse off than before his heart change. How can this be?

I was under the notion that if you are saved through the blood and redemptive process of Jesus Christ that one could not be *possessed* by a demon. The word *possession* shows *ownership*. While a believer is under the possession of the Holy Spirit in Christ, he can be *oppressed* (externally) or demonized (internally), as represented by the Demoniac in Mark chapter 5, by the enemy if his house is not in order as portrayed in the Matthew 12:45 example.

Understanding this was a game changer for me. It helped me to grasp why so many believers struggle in their sin and never come to the place where God wants them. They are literally bound by the enemy and do not fully comprehend how to beat the demons or what tools are needed to do it. They are *bound* by the strongman under Mark 3:27, unaware of the demonic realm and how they can work on a believer to make them ineffective in God's kingdom. I was that person.

I had no idea of the bondage I was under nor the Jezebel's influence on my life. It was time to kick out these hoards once and for all and to start living the life God had ordained for me. I had wasted enough time, and my mess is my ministry. It was time to kick Satan to the curb for good!

In August of 2012, I had a dream about an encounter

with Satan. Satan was sitting on a couch in front of me as I pulled out a gun to shoot him. I fired three times, and each time, only bubbles came out of the gun, rendering Satan into a fit of mocking laughter toward me. I could not kill him, and he knew it. The following weekend after a Sunday service at a local church, I was baptized for the third time. I never fully understood the concept of baptism nor the implications false baptisms can have on people's lives.

The week after my baptism, I had another dream. This was a dream of the real Ouija board experience I had in ninth grade with my girlfriends. We thought at the time that it was innocent and only played that one time. How wrong I was! In the dream, I saw a demonic entity enter my body as I was playing with the Ouija board. I remember telling the demon to leave me in the name of Jesus! I immediately went from a sleeping state into a woken state with zero control over my voice. As I was awakened, God was enabling me to speak the words over and over, "I command you in the name of Jesus, to leave me! I kept speaking the words over and over, completely unaware that I was not in control of my own voice and that the Lord was indeed in control over my words.

I felt like a pressure coming from my abdomen out of my mouth at that point. I felt light as a feather and finally freed from the bondage that had ensnared me for all those years! I did not know at that time this deliverance was the Jezebel spirit, but subsequent physical clues helped me to understand what had truly happened to me.

My endometriosis suddenly disappeared almost overnight. Behaviors and mindsets that had plagued me for years were suddenly gone. I was able to communicate with God on a deeper level, and my level of concentration for my relationship with the Lord was magnified one hundredfold. I started studying everything I could about the Jezebel spirit and how it had affected me my whole life. I had been set free, and God had paved the way for me to become an expert on this spirit -- how it seeks to destroy the church. I was more determined than ever to expose this enemy and help people live lives free from the bondage of this manifestation.

134

Chapter 34

Counseling 101

"Truly I tell you, whatever you bind on earth
will be bound in heaven, and whatever you lose on earth
will be loosed in heaven"
Matthew 18:18 NIV

Doug and I spent lots of time discussing the Jezebel spirit, what it was, and how it was destroying the church. Through careful prayer and showing him the scripture to support it, Doug understood his role in the divorce and what needed to be done to break the spiritual bondage his wife was under. I taught him to bind demonic spirits in the name of Jesus, fast for his wife, and fight for his marriage. It gave him a newfound energy to stand in the gap for his wife and how to fight the enemy with the Ephesians 6 armor of God.

Doug continued to battle every day and often stayed at home every weekend, so the enemy wouldn't have the opportunity to lead him astray. He was steadfast in his fight for his wife and continued his fight and sanctification for many months to follow.

In October 2018, Doug had lots of dreams about his wife, who was still pursuing the divorce. She wanted nothing to do with him. I asked Doug to record his dreams, assuring him his wife would return. "Trust the Lord with all your heart," I would say. Doug continued to struggle with this faith, but I continued to reassure him of God's promises and that his dreams pointed to his wife's return.

Doug was planning on visiting friends again in South

Carolina in December 2018. He asked if I wanted to get together for a few days over the New Year's Holiday. I figured he was harmless and because he was dedicated with reuniting with his wife, I agreed it would be a great opportunity for some face-to-face counseling. We could dive into the Word more instead of on the phone. When we initially met face-to-face, he was much taller than I expected. He was almost 6'5", and I am 5'0." After sharing a few dinners together, Doug invited me to a nice steak restaurant on New Year's Eve. As this restaurant was one of my favorites, we had a great time laughing and celebrating the New Year.

After Doug returned home, we continued the counseling, diving deeper into the Spiritual realm and helping him to understand the traits of the Jezebel spirit. Although he was stubborn at times, he was open to change and deeply wanted what the Lord wanted for him. He explained that he always wanted to do full-time ministry, but his wife laughed at him whenever he approached her about it. This behavior made sense as one of the chief goals of the Jezebel spirit is to destroy ministry; Doug was a prime target.

Doug continued his divorce battle, not giving the enemy any ground right through the winter of 2019. The divorce was final in April 2019, which perplexed him. He had whole-heartedly believed God would heal his marriage. I encouraged him to stay the course and wait -- God would indeed heal his relationship and that his ex-wife would eventually return.

In the meantime, Doug started his own church in New Hampshire. He refrained from dating while waiting for his ex-wife to return. When he did try to date using online dating sites, the Lord closed all opportunities for meeting someone. Aware of his loneliness and desire to find someone special, I kept encouraging him to wait and exercise the type of faith I'd taught him to have.

During the winter of 2019, Doug planned a visit to his

parents' home in South Florida to spend the Christmas holiday. He asked me to join him for New Year's and usher in 2020. He planned on staying a week at a hotel near my home. We returned to my favorite steakhouse for New Year's and enjoyed another great time. It was apparent, Doug's decision was to move ahead with his life. I also knew he liked me. Sadly, I had zero interest in him although I thoroughly enjoyed his company. He was non-threatening, a great friend, and I knew I could trust him -- no matter what.

We hung out together that week, and I showed him my favorite spots. I decided to invite him for one of my favorite Southern-cooked meals. He was drawing closer to me, but I kept my *friend's-only* position, squelching all his advances, which bothered me. Doug was such a great man and obvious *catch*, but he wasn't for me.

So, Doug returned to New Hampshire, and I prepared to move from a rental into my next home. At the time, I was working a fifty-hours-a-week job and finding it grueling to juggle work and care for my family.

Chapter 35

Healing with Hope

"Hope deferred makes the heart sick,
but a longing fulfilled is a tree of life.
Proverbs 13:12 NIV

A few months later I received a long email from Doug. It was an email that took me by surprise and off-guard. He explained he was over his ex-wife and was officially moving on from the whole ordeal. Doug was no longer interested in her or anything she had to offer him. He fully understood the Jezebel spirit, where she was spiritually, and what it had taken for her to leave and divorce him the way she did. What she did was evil, and even though Doug was moving on, I was convinced through what the Lord had shown me, the Almighty would indeed heal the relationship, reuniting these two people. Because of all Doug had experienced, his dreams, and the similarities to Hope, I was convinced the Lord would honor Doug's commitment to Him and reward his efforts.

Doug professed his undying love for me and had been denying it for some time. He was committed and transparent about his plans for me and what his intentions were. Although I thought Doug was handsome, I wasn't physically attracted to him. His note made me feel uncomfortable; I didn't feel the same way. He was Doug, my friend, my counselee, and someone I never looked at differently. I knew I needed to distance myself from him. I didn't want to give him any leverage into my life any more than he already had. So, we continued having our professional relationship, but I realized I was pulling away from him and explained numerous times we would never be together. God had placed me in Doug's life to help reconcile the marriage and refine his faith in Christ – nothing more.

Once again in March 2020, Doug invited me to visit him in South Florida where his parents lived, which he'd done numerous times over the past two years. He had to go down for a personal training certification. He'd pay all my expenses with no strings attached and no monkey business. "It will be good for you to get away. We can just enjoy a break from the bump and grind of life."

Oddly enough, I'd quit my stressful job the week before, so I truly needed a few days of rest and relaxation. I contemplated going as I trusted him, he was safe, and I really needed a few days of rest and relaxation. So, I accepted his invitation, flew to Ft. Lauderdale, and checked into a beautiful hotel in Boca Raton, Florida

We spent lots of time together, walked on the beach, collected seashells, ate at cool restaurants, and discussed life. I was uneasy. Here I was with this Godly man. He pursued Christ, possessed many of the qualities I wanted in a spouse, already loved me unconditionally, was caring, gracious, tall, and handsome, but I wasn't interested at all. His stares made me nervous, so I kept up the wall, keeping him at arm's length. He wasn't the man for me, and I refused to budge.

Chapter 36

"Penny Lover"

"The LORD God said, 'It is not good for the man to be alone.
I will make a helper suitable for him."
Genesis 2:18 NIV

This would be a great place to share Doug's dreams about he and I getting married. Before Christmas of 2019, Doug had a sneaking suspicion that our counseling relationship was more about God bringing us together as a couple, but in His timing and His way. Since I wasn't giving him any hope to which he could cleave, he asked the Lord for a dream or a sign confirming what he felt deep inside his heart. God not only answered but answered with the best dream Doug could have ever imagined- a dream of us married. Then one dream turned into two and then three dreams of us happily ever after. He dreamt of us at an old age sitting in rocking chairs, happily married. Then there was the dream of us holding hands before the throne of God, meeting Him in heaven. Doug shared these dreams with me and although I dismissed them, I knew they were a message from God.

It wasn't until the last night together, during my visit to Florida, that God flipped the switch for Doug in my heart. During my trip we spent time walking on the beach, eating ice cream, making faces and taking funny filtered pictures together while laughing hysterically. Before I retired to my room, Doug played Lionel Richie's song, "Penny Lover." He asked me to dance, so I complied, giving him the sideways *friends* dance hold. I was determined to keep him at a safe distance.

After we said goodnight, I began to second guess exempting him from my life. This is when the tables turned, and I suddenly began feeling love for him. It was God. There is no other way to explain the miracle that occurred in my heart. Only God could have turned this water into wine. Only God could have raised my dead heart to life.

I'd constructed walls between us for so long, never realizing the entire experience with Doug had been about us – not about him returning to his ex-wife. God had pulled off the improbable and seemingly impossible, an incredible *bait and switch* to fool the enemy and throw him off our trail. I knew deep in my heart God had put this wonderful man into my life. The Lord had prepared and designed him just for me. My stubborn heart and hurtful pattern of broken relationships had caused me to believe being alone was the best way to serve the Lord. But the enemy had deceived me. Doug was perfect for me, and I apologized to him that it had taken so long for him to break down my walls. I understood the Lord's timing was perfect and I was eager to see where He was going to bring us and our life together.

***

Because of Covid, Doug was forced to shut his personal training business for three weeks. This enabled him to travel to North Carolina and for us to spend quality time together. We really got to know each other as we experienced a trying three weeks moving my family and settling into our new home. Doug was an incredible partner during the whole move, working tirelessly to help me and the kids.

His love for me was obvious. Doug never swayed from giving me time to catch up with him as God continued to show me this was indeed the man I would grow old with. Our time over the past two years had established a strong friendship, so it was an easy transition to dating. God was expanding my heart toward Doug. Something beautiful was being orchestrated, and I trusted God with whatever He wanted for Doug and me.

At the end of the three-week visit, we knew this had been God-ordained time, and we knew God's hand was over the entire relationship, where it was going, and we trusted His plan.

Chapter 37

Going to the Courthouse

"He who finds a wife finds what is good
and receives favor from the LORD"
Proverbs 18:22 NIV

As spring blossomed in its glory, Doug and I had spent time praying, talking, and getting to know each other on a deeper level. I finally understood God had put us together despite my reluctancy to do so.

On May 22, I asked Doug, "Do you want to get married this morning?" I've never seen a human being move faster than this man that morning. It was as if he'd been struck by lightning! We knew in our hearts the Lord had brought us together. Our entire friendship and relationship had been a series of signs, dreams, answered prayer, and Divine Intervention. And we knew God was not finished with our story. We were waiting for a sign from God, so we both agreed we would go to the courthouse, and if we couldn't find two witnesses, we would wait to get married.

We arrived at the city's courthouse and were giggling like two teen-agers. That's when two-armed security guards approached us. After hearing our request, a few seconds later, they agreed to be our two witnesses. Talk about humor! The Lord had supplied us with armed protection, symbolizing the warfare against the enemy we were both going into with our marital covenant and vision for ministry. It is like the Lord was saying, "I got you Doug and Paige! Fear not, for I AM with you both!"

On May 22, 2020, Doug and I exchanged vows and sealed our covenant with one another. I couldn't believe this journey with Doug, but the Lord convinced me Doug was the man I'd seen in my dreams during my visit with God so many years before. It was a beautiful ending to all my years of searching and waiting, the questions I had, and the plan He had laid out for me. Although I felt more like this was an arranged marriage by the Lord Himself, my love for Doug was growing day by day.

Doug officially moved to North Carolina the first week of August 2020 with his truck full of his belongings, his handsome best friend Ben-Ben, a Newfie mix with a heart of gold, and a new beginning that God had prepared for him. We were both excited to be together and about everything God had been preparing in our hearts for over twenty years.

Next came yet another powerful dream. Doug had a dream about us opening a church together. It wasn't long before he was given yet another dream about us winning the lottery in the amount of one hundred thirty-nine million dollars. In the dream we led a church, and it was super important for us to spend the money in the right way without excessive purchases. We bought a house, paying cash for it, but via the discernment and leadership of the Holy Spirit.

Although I had stepped away from full-time ministry, I knew this was my sign that it was time to return. I knew after the visitation from God in 2002 my future would be spent serving Him in a full-time capacity. But the time of preparation was much longer than I had expected. My individual women's ministry began in 2011 and continued through 2015-16 as previously mentioned, but my sabbatical was ending, and it was time to return now as a married couple in Christ's service. Doug and I began brainstorming about the ministry, where it would be, and what it would look like. We had similar goals, a strong passion for others, and we were equally yoked spiritually. I never understood what truly being *equally yoked* meant until I met Doug. Equally yoked does not mean marrying or dating someone that qualifies just because they call themselves a *Christian*. I always thought if they were *Christian*, we were equally yoked; how wrong I was. I had always needed a mature believer who loved the Lord, exemplified the fruits of the Spirit according to Galatians 5, and would love his wife according to the Ephesians 5 mandate. Doug met them all, and he was the first to fill all the qualities I needed.

So, we hired a commercial real estate broker who passionately searched for the exact place we needed to start our ministry. In October 2020, we found our place and NUMA Ministries was born.

Chapter 38

NUMA

"The wind blows where it wishes, and you hear its sound, but
you do not know where it comes from or where it goes. So, it
is with everyone who is born of the Spirit."
John 3:8 ESV

NUMA means *spirit wind* in the Greek language. It is such
a fitting name for our new endeavor. I had contemplated
the name over the last four years, originally choosing the
name for my dance fitness studio, but it never filled the
true intention of what the Lord was showing me. Doug and
I both agreed that the old way of doing church, the mega
church model, and all its self-promotion, hyper-grace, strict
dogma, tradition, and entertainment were on the way out.
The original Acts church that God designed for discipleship
training was on the move. We knew God's vision for our lives
would never come to fruition without breaking free from this
institution of church and proclaiming the Gospel free and
clear of institutional confinements.

Our new place was small but perfect for our start. We
wanted an office for Biblical counseling, a back room (sound-
proof) for my recording studio, and a medium sized room for
our Sunday service. Doug had an extensive background in
construction. So, our complete renovation started on October
3, 2020 with a full gutting of the interior.

We knew the enemy would throw up obstacles so
this place wouldn't happen. For the next twelve weeks, he
threw everything possible to frustrate our plans and keep

us from finishing. Any and all projects that would normally take hours turned into days. As frustrated as Doug was, he never faltered and fought his way through each and every problem that arose. Boy, did they come up! He went over and beyond to make our new place as inviting and warm as possible, keeping a key eye to detail while trying to keep us honorable to our budget. It was easy to see the enemy working against us, and just proved to Doug and me that we were on point with the Lord's leading. God wanted us to press forward no matter what. It is a glorious thing to know that you are perfectly in the Lord's will, despite the troubles and persecutions faced along the way. There is no greater joy than to understand where you stand and that God is in perfect control of the situation.

As each week passed, Doug received a *download* from the Lord regarding our topic for each Sunday. He said it was like God was writing the sermons for us to present each week. Doug and I had discussed in detail that we wanted to be a church that is truly led by the Holy Spirit in all things. At some point I will write at length on this topic, but for the sake of brevity I will just say that the American Gospel has been backed by a business model instead of the leading of God's Spirit.

We know the church paradigm in America is dying from a concoction of *feel-good* sermons and *unoffensive doctrinal* messages. The seriousness of sin and especially repentance is far removed from the light shows and prosperity messages seen in so many churches today. On the other hand, another type of church exists. It's one with a strict, legalistic set of rules, devoid of the Holy Spirit, and deep on indoctrination and fear. Both styles are contrary to the original church in 1 Corinthians 14 and spiritual gifted church of 1 Corinthians 12. The institution of church today (not all, but corporately speaking) is deep in maintaining its members or numbers to support the massive amounts of money to keep their concert halls open and salaries paid, they have lost their focus: Christ and making disciples of all nations. Numbers don't mean blessings. God wants an army trained for battle, not a stadium filled with smoke machines and amen corners.

Deified leaders giving three-point feel-good sermons must devolve into a repentant, Spirit filled assembly with people on fire for the kingdom of God. Jesus spoke of money and demons more than anything else during his public ministry. We must go and do the same. We must be the vessels by which God sets the captives free and then fill them with the Holy Spirit. There are many captive Christians who aren't battling against the enemy because they don't understand how he operates in their lives. Little did I know, so many years ago, that I would be extensively trained in spiritual warfare. Little did I know NUMA would be born. If it weren't for trusting the leadership of the Holy Spirit through dreams and visions given during that season, Doug and I would not have moved in God's unction.

I recall sharing about how the Holy Spirit leads with Doug. I told him our lives would be drastically different than that which he was accustomed. He was one for stability and knowing the next move he would make. Doug is a planner. When led by the Spirit of God, He marks out our paths- not us. We may try to plan our ways, but in the end, if we are truly surrendered to Him, our steps are ordered by Him. And true to my word, right after we married, God began giving Doug dreams about NUMA. He would give a dream, then we would take the step. He would give another dream, and we would take another step.

NUMA is growing today, but she is growing upward more than outward. This upward growth is according to Ephesians 4:11-14. The gifts of the Lord are given so that the church would be matured and lacking nothing. They are given so that we will not be tossed and blown about by every wind of new teaching. NUMA doesn't offer anything new, per se. God is using us to break out of the old way and into the new! That is why our tag line phrase is, "The wind of change."

The Lord always told me, "Paige, faith is the key." He is always right.

Chapter 39

Fear of the Lord

"The Spirit of the LORD will rest on him— the Spirit of wisdom
and of understanding, the Spirit of counsel and of might, the
Spirit of the knowledge and fear of the LORD—"
Isaiah 11:2 NIV

According to King Solomon, "The fear of the Lord is the
beginning of knowledge," and he also said, "The fear of the
Lord is the hatred of evil" (Proverbs. 1:7, 8:13). David said,
"Let all the earth fear the Lord; let all the inhabitants of the
world stand in awe of him" (Psalm 33:8). I now have a great
understanding of the fear of the Lord. That fear was initiated
during my visit with God and the life review I witnessed
and now reflect upon daily. Subsequently, this fear is one
of reverence and not the fear I experienced throughout my
life that was instilled by the enemy. This reverence stands
in awe and appreciation of the One in which all power and
majesty resides.

As of 2022, twenty years would pass before I realized
my experience of Hell and glimpse of heaven was much
more than anything I could have ever imagined. Parts of it
would also reflect a future period of my journey when I would
feel as though the Lord had forsaken me. To put it another
way, back then, I did not know the depth in which the Lord
would communicate. Remember, I had not read the Bible nor
had any real experience with God other than going to church
and crying out to Him when in trouble. I thought I was being
punished for my rebellion against God, so He showed me a

vision of Hell! My experience was so much more than that!

Years later, one of my seminary professors would share about how the Lord spoke "to and through" His prophets or certain individuals in scripture. A Biblical example would be Ezekiel writing to an actual historical person, the king of Tyre, while also speaking far beyond a human leader to the dateless past with a description of the original fall of Lucifer.

Then this message came to me from the Lord: "Son of man, give the prince of Tyre this message from the Sovereign Lord: 'In your great pride you claim, 'I am a god! I sit on a divine throne in the heart of the sea.' But you are only a man and not a god, though you boast that you are a god." (Ezekiel 28:1-2)

And then again, he says, "Sing this funeral song for the king of Tyre. Give him this message from the Sovereign Lord: 'You were the model of perfection, full of wisdom and exquisite in beauty. You were in Eden, the garden of God. Your clothing was adorned with every precious stone' and then proceeds to name the stones." (Ezekiel 28:11-13)

Again, while speaking to the present, God refers to the past. In my case, God spoke to the present and the future. Later, I would virtually live out moments from that Hell experience in 2002. For example, while in Hell, as I briefly explained earlier, I saw my boyfriend, who would eventually be my husband and father to my son. He didn't say a word unless I tried to approach him.

One day, as I was praying, the Lord revealed why this happened, telling of this future relationship between my boyfriend and me. I knew the Hell experience was a *too and through*, multi-faceted, multi-layered depiction of then and now. Although the Lord used the experience to convey His message in 2002, it was filled with future meaning and purpose. Unfortunately, that boyfriend and I married and divorced seven years later. Looking back, I see the fullness

151

of our relationship. During the visitation he would represent a demonic bondage with which I would face off in the future. I have learned the hard way that our Hell on earth is what we make it because of the company we keep, the choices we make, and the relationships we cultivate.

Christians who journey with the Holy Spirit will also experience a *too and through* measure of God's prophetic utterances. Isaiah fifty-three speaks of the Suffering Servant. There was a then and not yet fulfillment. King David was also notorious for 'too and through' prophecies.

Chapter 40

Sanctification

"It is God's will that you should be sanctified:
that you should avoid sexual immorality"
1 Thessalonians 4:3 NIV

Sanctification is the process of becoming more like Christ by purifying our hearts and minds through repentance, prayer, and spiritual practices. God began my sanctification process as an alcoholic or addict follows a twelve-step program. This is the same concept and paradigm God brought me through.

Surrender is first, understanding what *not my will* but *your will* really means. As in the step-by-step program, God told me I needed to *truly* forgive everyone, which we know can be hard to do. Sometimes, we think we've forgiven someone but we haven't. It's important to remember that we are told in Hebrews 12:15 that the root of bitterness, if allowed to grow, will trouble us, and possibly cause defilement. The core of unforgiveness is bitterness. I recognized my bitterness and wanted to extract that root of bitterness from my heart and soul once and for all. So, God led me to write letters – even if they were never mailed.

I'd have a dream, like the one I had about my paternal grandmother. My dream was about the bitterness (unforgiveness) I felt toward her. In obedience to what the Lord was telling me to do, I wrote a letter to her, baring my heart and hurts she had caused me. I wrote everything on paper that I would have said if she had been alive. Afterwards, I tore it up and didn't regress or tried not to. As humans, we can't forget what someone did, but we have to be careful not to harbor bitterness toward anyone. Writing letters and releasing bitterness was part of the healing process not only for me but many I would counsel over the years as well.

Then I had to forgive my stepfathers. I wrote a letter to the stepfather who had sexually abused me all those years – the fourth one – the main one. In the letter I stated, "You stole my childhood, my virginity, two precious things, which I can never get. But I forgive you, and I pray for your salvation. You were a deacon in the church, serving the Lord, and I hope the end turns out well for you."

I never received a response, but I discovered years later he was following me on my *Facebook* ministry page. Joyce Meyer set an example for me. She was able to forgive her father and knew her mother was aware of the abuse. But the Lord had her care for her parents. Her situation was horrific. This man was her biological father, so at least I didn't have to be around my stepfather anymore. Just know that this process of forgiveness went on for a while. Forgiveness was really big then, and it still is. But there was restoration after it. This is an important part of the sanctification process.

The majority of Christians don't allow the full measure of sanctification to be done in their lives. They don't understand sanctification and look at it as "God is coming after me," especially if their view of God is angry and judicial. "God is sending this to me." "What have I done?" "Why is God putting me through this?" They begin viewing with filters on. "I must have disobeyed the Lord." "I'm being attacked so much." "Obviously, there is something I'm not doing." "Is this a test?" "Is this a trial?" "Is this the dark night of the soul?" "Am I going through the refiner's fire?" "Does the enemy have a legal right to me?"

They must ask themselves if there is something generationally where the door is open, giving the enemy a right to harass them. Satan had to ask permission to torment Job, but what people usually don't see in the book of *Job* other than he had patience and endured so much, thus the adage "patience of Job," is Job's pride. It took almost forty-two chapters for Job to realize he was a sinner, he was guilty, and he needed to repent. Once he did that, everything changed. The power of repentance is huge. As Christians, when we're under attack, it is very difficult to parse that out. That is one thing the Lord has taught me to do and taught me to help others to be able to do -- understand why they are going through what they are going through.

We are always in the sanctification process. It begins with forgiveness, repentance, and ensuring your side of the porch is clean. Then you proceed from there. The Lord really worked with me for quite some time, person after person. "We'll deal with this situation and then restoration will come."

After all of that, I dreamt about the gentleman who physically abused me so badly in that almost four-year relationship. I hadn't dreamt about him for years. But every time I dreamt of him; I would experience a spiritual attack afterwards. When the Lord taught me about dreams, I realized this was the evil spirit that came in through that relationship. It was so beautiful how He restored me in that area.

To give you a quick synopsis, we went through forgiveness, with Him teaching me about sanctification. Then there was restoration. Just as God does with nations and will do with Israel. He does it on an individual level. The ex-boyfriend who had physically abused me and contacted me, so he could say he was sorry is an excellent example of restoration. I had prayed about it and received confirmation this was real. Eventually, the spiritual attacks will leave once restoration comes.

This is trauma, and the only way to heal trauma is to replace it with love. So, remember that I went and met him?

His apology was tearful. He also said, "You were the one who got away." His remarks were so restorative. This was the redemption I needed for that situation. Finally, I was able to close that chapter in my life entirely.

I was reminded of the wit, charm, and charisma of God, that I'd known well in 2002. Everyday, I long to have a smidgeon of that in my day. I was able to see my Heavenly Father take care of business. It was great! He did that in many situations. He restored one by one. But, first, it required the threshing floor and really allowing the sanctification process. With most Christians, the process begins, but they don't know what it is. They aren't taught about the process and why they are going through different things. You hear messages of salvation, teachings of the word, but not enough about the sanctification process, which is another of my areas of specialty. I've trained others to understand the process, as well as helping them through the process.

Epilogue

It has been twenty years since my visitation from the Lord. It was a two-week span I will never forget, and one that changed the course of my life forever. As I reflect on my former life, I shudder at the thought of where I would have ended up had the Lord not interceded and rescued me. Over the years, I have received many of the promises God showed me during my visit with Him, and I look forward to the others that haven't manifested yet.

I know the completion of this book (my testimony) is not the end of the call on my life. To tell you the truth, I could fill several more pages with moments from the Lord's special visit with me, but the time will come to share the other details. We are living in such a time that the Holy Spirit is pouring His glory on flesh like never before. It brings joy in my life to hear the testimony of God's children, and I hope you were blessed by reading mine as well.

Over the last year, I have had many prophetic dreams and visions. The dreams are connecting with events in my life or the lives of those for whom I have prayed. But more than anything else I am seeing people set free from demonic bondages.

Today "Christians" are missing out on a deep personal relationship with Jesus because their temples are defiled. I believe much of the church has left her true love in order to be more seeker friendly. Individuals in the church are not rooted in the word of God, therefore cannot move beyond the entrance to the door of Christianity. They waste so much time battling the enemy and the same repetitive sin patterns that they never grow into their gifting, and fulfill what God had ordained for them. The early church understood the biblical mandate to not only make disciples of all nations, but to heal the sick, raise the dead, cleanse the Leapers, *and cast out demons.* Nothing changed. Jesus did not change his mind. Instead, the church moved away from this mandate and replaced it with what the culture demanded. We need another reformation in the church. This time, however, it needs to be radically transformed, cleansed of defilement, and prepared to be used in the end time harvest.

My hope is that you grow into who God has ordained you to be. I pray this book has opened your eyes to the spiritual realm, the realities of life after death, and that our choices have eternal repercussions. If you have given up hope or think that your situation is far from redeemable, consider what God has done for me.

Know this, I had considered removing some of the descriptive language used to portray the early days of my traumatic life. I told my husband that Christians may be offended by the graphic details I used. However, he said that everyone has a story, and you need to know that no matter what has happened to you, God will redeem you. The enemy wants us to dumb down our stories as not to offend anyone, but you need to know the truth, no matter how ugly it is. And in all honestly, I only shared a portion of the horrors I faced. If He gave me beauty for ashes, He will do the same for you. I may not know you, but I know God. What the enemy uses to harm you, God will use to bless you. He is the hope of glory! Don't give up! Don't give in! Keep on keeping on because it's not how you start, its how you finish! Finish strong my brothers and sisters. I love you all!

God Bless,

Paige Coffey